DESPERATE
MEASURES

.MURDEROUS MATHS.

JOIN THE MURDEROUS MATHS GANG FOR MORE FUN, GAMES AND TIPS AT www.murderousmaths.co.uk

DESPERATE
MEASURES

KJARTAN POSKITT

Illustrated by
Philip Reeve

With special thanks to Marilyn Malin who is both an inspirational friend and a razor-sharp agent.

Scholastic Children's Books,
Euston House, 24 Eversholt Street,
London NW1 1DB, UK
a division of Scholastic Ltd
London ~ New York ~ Toronto ~ Sydney ~ Auckland
Mexico City ~ New Delhi ~ Hong Kong

Published by Scholastic Ltd 2000

Text copyright © Kjartan Potkitt 2000
Illustrations copyright © Philip Reeve 2000

10 digit ISBN 0 439 01370 4
13 digit ISBN 978 0439 01370 3

Typeset by TW Typesetting, Midsomer Norton, Somerset
Printed and bound by Nørhaven Paperback A/S, Denmark

15 17 19 20 18 16

The right of Kjartan Poskitt and Philip Reeve to be identified as the
author and illustrator of this work respectively has been asserted by them
in accordance with the Copyright, Designs and Patents Act, 1988.

CONTENTS

DON'T MESS WITH MEASUREMENTS

Yes, welcome to one of the most murderous bits of maths – the weird and wonderful world of measurements.

Even when you were only 10 minutes old measurements started to rule your life because you immediately got weighed. (This was so that all the gushing grannies and aunties had something sensible to talk about instead of coming up with drivel like "Oh look, she's got Uncle Mark's nose".) Measurements continue to interfere with your life until the day they fit you for a long wooden box.

You can't avoid them, you can't ignore them and most of all you can't mess about with them, as this story from police files shows:

City: **Chicago, Illinois, U.S.A.**
Place: **The Penthouse Suite, Glitz Hotel**
Date: **13 March, 1930**
Time: **11:23 p.m.**

"Will you stop staring like I'm some sort of freak or something," said the lady with the tall rabbit ears. "I'm back on in three minutes, so get a move on!"

"You should remember who's the boss here," drawled Blade Boccelli, but the six other men, scattered around the darkened apartment, stayed silent. Dolly Snowlips wasn't the sort to be intimidated, even if she did have long quivering whiskers glued to her cheeks.

"And you should remember who fixed this whole operation," she snapped. "Who got the job as the Easter bunny for the Stonyguy Arts Foundation dinner? Who sneaked the keys to this apartment? And who planned how we're gonna get away with one million bucks worth of picture?"

"I still don't see how one lousy picture can be worth a million bucks," said the Weasel.

"Yeah," said Chainsaw Charlie. "If that's what pictures cost, how come we're robbing them rather than painting them?"

"Because you didn't die in Europe three hundred years ago," said Dolly. "Now you know what you got to do. The room with the picture is six floors below this one, and each floor is four metres high."

"That makes twenty-four metres," said the thin man.

"Numbers is right," said the Weasel. "Only we don't know how long a metre is."

"It's this new French thing from Paris, France," said Dolly tossing a tape measure over. "This tape is

one metre long, so use it to cut yourselves twenty-four metres worth of rope, drop somebody down the side of the building, in they climb and make smart with the art."

"Did you say rope?" asked One Finger Jimmy.

"Yeah, a rope," said Dolly. "You did bring a rope, didn't you?"

The six men all turned to look at Blade who was very glad the lights were out.

"We don't need no rope," said Blade trying to sound clever.

"Oh right!" sneered Dolly. "And I suppose one of you guys thinks he can hover himself half a mile above the sidewalk without one. This I gotta see."

"Ain't it time you were dishing out your little candy eggs?" snapped Blade.

"I guess," said Dolly. "But remember, rope or no rope, when we meet at Luigi's later I expect you to be holding one million bucks worth of paint."

With an arrogant twitch of her rabbit tail she was gone.

"So which one of us can fly, Blade?" asked Porky.

"It sure ain't you," sniggered the Weasel. "With your size it'd be easier to move the window up to you than lower you down."

In less than a second the big man was jamming Weasel's head into the waste-paper bin.

"You let my brother go, or I'll pull the trigger," said Half-smile Gabrianni who seemed to have conjured his Dawson-Roach 98 from thin air. "He was just joking."

"Yeah, our brother's always joking," said Chainsaw. "He jokes all the time. In fact, come to think of it, we really hate it."

"That's true," nodded Half-smile. "On second thoughts, leave him in there or I'll pull the trigger."

"So how come you forgot to bring a rope, boss?" asked Jimmy.

"I didn't forget nothing," said Blade. "Suppose we were stopped and searched? What would they have found?"

"About a dozen shooters, a set of throwing knives, a grenade, half a bottle of cyanide, a chainsaw and enough dynamite to send Chicago over the lake to Canada," said Chainsaw.

"Yeah, but just suppose they'd found we were carrying a rope?" asked Blade. "That would have made us look suspicious."

"So what we gonna do?" asked Porky.

"We all need to take off our braces and belts," said Blade. "Then we tie them together in one long line."

After a lot of grumbling and fumbling, a long knotted trail of miscellaneous clothing was laid out along the floor.

"Numbers, you've checked it with the tape," said Blade. "What do you get?"

"Twenty-four metres exactly," said Numbers.

"Then that's perfect!" said Blade. "That leaves just one more thing to sort out. Who goes through the window?"

"Mmmm ... mmmm," came a sound from inside the waste bin.

"I think he's saying 'me me'," said Jimmy. "What does anybody else think?"

"Of course he is!" they all replied at once and hurried to remove the waste bin.

In a moment the Weasel was perched on the window ledge with the final belt in the line tied around under his armpits.

"Oh please, fellas," whimpered the Weasel. "Being this high up could kill a guy!"

"Whoever heard of height killing anybody?" said Jimmy.

"That's right," agreed Chainsaw. "It's not height that kills you. It's when you run out of height and hit the ground – that's what kills you."

"I've heard enough," said Blade. "Would somebody mind helping our chicken leave the nest?"

With a six-handed push Weasel was launched out into the night air.

"Ahhhhh...!" THUNK!

Six faces peered over the edge and saw that the small man had come to rest on a window ledge far below them. He shook his head, rubbed his eyes and then looked up. "Wow! That was awesome!" he grinned.

They carefully feed out the rest of the line. "OK," said Weasel, "How do I open the window?"

"Can't you kick it in?" Blade called down.

"It looks pretty tough," said Weasel. "But if you guys hold on tight, I'll swing myself out and crash in on it."

It was a real shame that Weasel couldn't see the faces of the others because just for once in his miserable life he had generated a wave of respect which almost bordered on hero-worship.

"Everybody hold tight on to that line with both hands," Blade ordered.

12

"But we need one hand free to hold our trousers up," said Half-smile. "Our belts and braces are all tied into that line."

"I said both hands and I meant it," said Blade choking back a tear. "That's one brave man down there and right now he's depending on us."

Slowly, one by one, each man reached out to put his second hand on the line and as each man did so his trousers silently slid down to his ankles. It was a very solemn moment.

"OK, Weasel," shouted Blade. "Give it your best shot!"

With a mightly kick the small man hurled himself away from the side of the building, and then with his feet braced forwards he started to swing back in again.

Place: Luigi's Diner, Upper Main Street
Time: 3 hours and 17 minutes later
"I don't want to hear this," said Dolly, "but tell it to me again anyway."

The seven men round the table stared gloomily into their pasta which had spent the last two hours congealing into rubber. Chainsaw was even wondering if he wouldn't have rather died in Europe holding a paintbrush three hundred years ago. At least he wouldn't be sitting here being lectured by a woman with drooping whiskers and crumpled furry ears.

"Are you sure you got your measurements right?" sighed Blade.

"Of course," snapped Dolly. "So how come the human baboon came smashing through a hotel window two floors below where he should have done? How come he slid straight across the dining table of the police department's annual dinner? How come we're all due to appear in court tomorrow morning?"

"Will you stop with the questions!" moaned Jimmy.

"Yeah, sure," snapped Dolly. "Just as soon as you guys start with the answers. Hey cookie-face, where you going?"

"I gotta use the men's room," said Half-smile rising to his feet and clutching his trousers.

"Gee whizz, Mr Gabrianni," chirped up Benni the waiter. "Something happen to your belt?"

"It got stretched," said Half-smile.

"Stretched?" asked Dolly. "What did you do with it? Lend it to buffalo-butt here?"

"I didn't borrow no belt," said Porky. "We all had to tie our belts and braces in the line."

"Line?" gasped Dolly. "What line?"

"Well you see," began Blade. "It was like this..."

But Dolly was way ahead of him.

"You mean to say that you knuckle heads measured twenty-four metres with your belts and elastic braces, and then hung rat-face out on the end of it all? Tell me I'm wrong."

The men shook their heads. Telling Dolly that she was wrong would have been madness even at the best of times, and this was definitely not the best of times. Dolly poured herself another glass of red.

"But the line definitely measured twenty-four metres," said Numbers. "I know about that sort of stuff."

"Of course the line measured twenty-four metres," sighed Dolly, "until his weight pulling down stretched it out. You don't mess about with measurements you dummies!"

"Well it all makes some sort of sense I suppose," said the Weasel. "Thanks to our stretching measurements, it looks like we'll all end up doing a stretch."

"There he goes making with the jokes again," said Chainsaw.

At least Benni laughed, but then they all turned to look at him.

So Benni quickly shut up.

HOW LONG IS A LINE?

Most of the measuring you'll ever have to do involves seeing how long something is and so, just for you, here is the secret method that has been handed down through thousands of generations...

Put a ruler or a tape measure next to the thing you're measuring.

It's so simple it's brilliant, especially if whatever you are measuring is an exact number of units long.

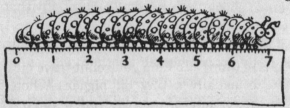

This sociable little caterpillar is being exactly 7 cm long, which is very kind of it. What a jolly helpful little chap he is. Sadly, though, the world is a cruel place and inevitably this sort of thing happens...

16

To take our minds off the savagery of nature, let's just check that we know exactly how rulers work. As well as big lines, rulers also have lots of smaller lines on them like this:

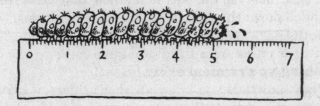

On this ruler the bigger lines are each exactly one centimetre apart, and the gap between them is divided into 10 "sub-divisions". This means that each small line indicates 0·1 of a centimetre (cm) or 1 millimetre (mm). (To help you count them out, the fifth line is usually a tiny bit bigger.) When you measure the remains of your caterpillar you put one end at the "0" and then see where the other end comes to. In the picture the caterpillar reaches all the way to the 5 cm mark, but then finishes at the third little line beyond. This means that it is 5·3 cm long.

Occasionally you'll come across a ruler that looks like this:

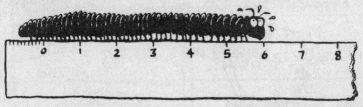

The ruler makers haven't bothered to put little lines all down the ruler, instead they've just put a little set of lines on the other side of the zero. To measure this centipede, you put one end on the "0" but then slide it backwards a little bit until the other end is exactly on one of the centimetre marks. In this case you can see that the centipede is 6 cm long *plus* seven of the little lines, which makes the centipede 6·7 cm long in total.

Your first practical experiment!

What fun! Now you know all about rulers, it's time to use this knowledge for the benefit of mankind, so let's get on with a really murderous measurement.

Don't panic – it's nothing like that. All you have to measure is how wide this book is, so just put a ruler across it and read off the answer.

You'll get an answer of 0·0001282567 kilometres.

If you're not happy with that, then another way of describing the width is 1282567000 angstroms. Or if you prefer, 0·0000000000000001350071 light-years. How's that?

Oh all right then. In millimetres you'll find the book is 128·2567 mm wide.

Of course that's the sensible answer but, as you can already see, measuring isn't quite as straight forward as it may seem. Even for the easiest measurements there are two things you have to do:

- Decide on the most suitable units to use.
- Work out how accurate you have to be.

The right units

The units you use should be of a similar "order of size" to what you are measuring, which means that they shouldn't be too big or too small. Although there's nothing actually wrong in giving the width of this book in kilometres, having loads of zeros looks pretty silly and what's more it's all too easy to miss one out or put an extra one in.

One kilometre is the same as *one thousand* metres, and so kilometres are used for measuring things like how far you're going on your holidays. So it's no wonder that they are far too big for measuring books properly and obviously millimetres are far too small to measure how far you're going on your holidays. (Unless you intend to spend an exhilarating week in August sitting slightly further along the sofa.)

DEAR MUM AND DAD,
HAVING A LOVELY
TIME AT THIS END.
WEATHER LOVELY.
WISH YOU WERE
HERE.

One light-year is the distance that light can travel in one year and, needless to say, light zooms along at a mindlessly irresponsible rate.

In just one year light can travel *9,500 million million* metres and so light-years are used to describe massive lengths such as the distances to far away stars and alien galaxies. That's why measuring this book in light-years looks even sillier than kilometres.

On the other hand an "angstrom" is equal to 0·0000000001 of a metre, or *one ten thousand millionth* of a metre. (You can even describe an angstrom as 10^{-10} m if you like. You'll see how that works later on.) Angstroms are used for measuring really tiny things like atoms and light waves, and they have a rather good sign: Å.

Metres themselves are in the order of book size, and you could well describe this book as being 0·13 metres across (0·13 m). However it's usually nicer to have some numbers in front of the decimal point. So, as there are 1,000 millimetres in one metre, you can say the width of the book is 130 mm. (Some people prefer to use centimetres, and as there are 100 cm to one metre, that gives the width of the book as 13 cm. There is a complete list of all the words like "kilo" "centi" and "milli" on page 47.)

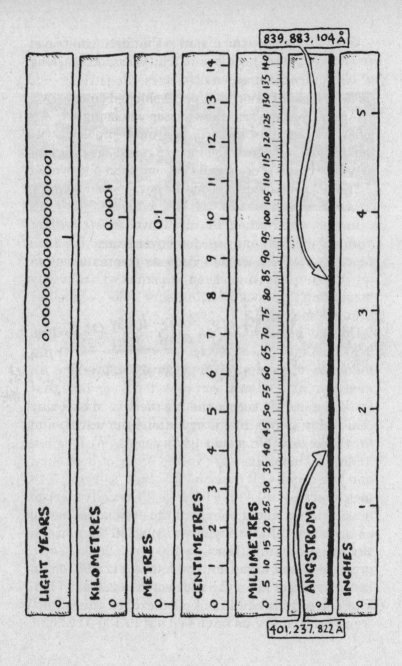

839,883,104 Å

401,237,822 Å

LIGHT YEARS

0.000000000000000001

KILOMETRES

0.0001

METRES

0.1

CENTIMETRES

MILLIMETRES

ANGSTROMS

INCHES

Here's a comparison of how big different units are. These seven scales are in light-years, kilometres, metres, centimetres, millimetres, angstroms and just for fun there's one in old-fashioned "inches".

Although there's nothing to stop you using any size of units you like, there is one more problem with having loads of zeros. You have to spend ages working out how many there should be, and then once you've written them all down people go goggle-eyed trying to count them up.

In fact even when *this* book was being written there was a right old punch up over how many zeros should have been in the light-year measurement we saw earlier, but as always the author was proved to be correct.

Good grief! It seems the Murderous Maths staff are creeping into the factory at night and scribbling in the books. What sad little people. We'll ignore them and move on.

Accuracy
Even if you could measure this book accurately enough to get the the width as 128·2567 mm, you're wasting your time. Here's why:
- It might get damp and swell out to 128·9874 mm.
- It might get hot and frizzle down to 127·4553 mm.
- Somebody is bound to get so excited turning the pages that it gets stretched out to 130·0112 mm.

- The edges will never be *perfectly* straight. Here's a close up of the edge of this book:

:er,

As you move down the book, the extra lumps and holes in the paper could affect the width as much as 0·5 mm which makes your measurement of 128·2567 mm rather pointless.

However the main reason for not giving so many figures is that NOBODY CARES.

So how many figures should you bother with? Well it all depends on what you are doing. If it's a brain transplant and you are fixing up all the tiny nerve endings then you have to be REALLY accurate and use measurements to the nearest millionth of a metre because if you wire brains up wrong the patient may end up kicking himself on the nose when he's trying to scratch his knee. On the other hand, if your hamster conks out and you're giving it a burial service, make the hole about a metre deep and that'll be close enough.

HONESTLY, I FEEL FINE!

For measuring this book, as we saw before, 130 mm seemed close enough. If you wanted to be a tiny bit more accurate you might have said it was 128 mm, but that will do! If you put any more figures on the end, it makes you look sad and pointless.

Of course there will always be one or two Murderous Maths readers who got carried away and who DID make an excruciatingly accurate measurement of the book. Although it seemed clever at the time, right now you'll be squirming with embarrassment but don't worry because help is at hand.

Looking cool and rounding off

Whatever you choose to do in life, there are some little gimmicks that you simply HAVE TO master otherwise you are simply not cool. For instance, if you play basketball then you're nothing if you can't spin the ball on the end of your finger. If you're a vicar then it's crucial that you can hold a cup of tea on a saucer, eat a sticky bun, shake hands with some aunties and stop the raffle tickets blowing away all at once.

Lumberjacks should never cry when they get splinters, junior doctors regard sleep as a sign of weakness and if you're a hamster then you're a social misfit unless you can stuff at least two weeks' supply of dinner in your cheeks. (A word of warning for hamsters – don't try to get three weeks of dinner in your cheeks. It might seem ultra cool, but remember you're only little. You just can't take it, and you'll end up in a hole about a metre deep.)

With maths there's no way you can walk tall strutting your stuff unless you've cracked "rounding off". This is the slick way of reducing how many numbers you've got in a measurement, but keeping what's left as accurate as possible. Rounding off is a complete art form in itself, and it includes such groovy things as "significant digits" and "relevant zeros" but there's no room for all that here, although you will find it in *The Essential Arithmetricks*.

For now, all you need to do is decide how many digits you need and replace the rest with zeros... BUT look at what the next digit would have been. If it would have been a "5" or more, then add one to your final digit. Let's have another look at our silly measurement:

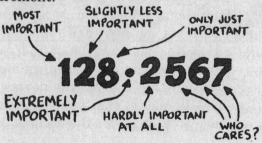

If you wanted to be reasonably accurate, you could just use the most important three digits and so end up with 128·0000 which is the same as 128. If you wanted to be very accurate, you would write down "128·3" because the first four digits are 128·2, but the next one would have been a 5, so you add 1 to the final 2. If you just wanted to give two significant digits, after rounding off you get 130.

If you're in any doubt, just imagine the measurement on a ruler.

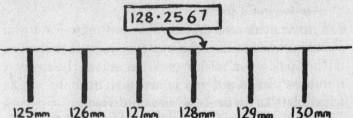

All you do is decide which mark is nearer to the exact measurement, and that's the one you need.

Degrees of accuracy – and the disappearing book!
Sometimes you get told how accurate measurements have to be, and to be posh this is called the "degree of accuracy". You might be told to give a measurement to "three significant digits" or maybe "two significant digits" or if you're a brain surgeon "ten significant digits", so all you do is write down the number of digits you need and round off as we saw before. However, it's more likely that you are told to give a measurement to "the nearest metre" or "the nearest millimetre" or even "the nearest light-year". This usually means that your measurement should not have anything after the decimal point.

Let's have a final look at the width of this book again... In millimetres it was 128·2567 mm. Let's see what it is...

- ...to the nearest millimetre. It's 128 mm. Easy!
- ...to the nearest centimetre. If the book is 128 mm wide, then it is 12·8 cm wide, but we round this up to 13 cm.
- ...to the nearest 10 mm. This is the same as working to the nearest 1 cm, but doing it in millimetres with a zero in the units column. In this case we get 130 mm.
- ...to the nearest metre. This is funny. First you convert the millimetre measurement to metres so the book is 0·1282567 m. What is it to the nearest metre? In other words we just need a "whole number" of metres – so as we said before, you don't want anything after the decimal point. This means that to the *nearest* metre, this book is 0 m wide. Wow – this means that you've just performed the amazing disappearing book trick!
- ...to the nearest light-year. This is too silly to think about.
- ...to the nearest angstrom. This is also rather silly but if anybody is piggish enough to ask for the width in angstroms, you've got three choices:
  1 Go to a massive physics laboratory with the right equipment and measure it. (Yawn.)
  2 Tell them to get lost.
  3 Bluff. If you convert the original measurement to angstroms you get 1,282,567,000 Å but the last three zeros show you haven't measured it properly. To make it look exact, just add on a couple more to get 1,282,567,002 Å. If anyone

suspects that you've just made it up, they can't do anything about it unless they go and measure it themselves. Ha ha ha, serves them right.

● ...to the nearest *half* mm. Occasionally for a bit of extra accuracy, you might be asked to work to half a unit. This means rather than always giving a round number, your answer might have a 0·5 on the end. Use your common sense to decide if 128·2567 mm is closer to 128·0 mm or 128·5 mm? Let's look at a ruler again:

It's very slightly closer to the 128·5 mm mark, so that's the answer you should give.

There, that's the basic mechanics of measuring a line dealt with. As you can see it just takes a bit of common sense and you can give measurements to the right degree of accuracy in the correct size of units for anything. Of course there are all sorts of units for measuring all sorts of different things and it's vital that you make it clear what sort you are using, as you're about to find out.

PECKS, PALMS, PINTS AND PENNYWEIGHTS
... or how many hands does a horse need?

Suddenly desperate times are upon you. You need to get some money and so you do the most obvious thing – you decide to sell your bath. Somebody phones up and asks you six questions, but you get the answers muddled up.

HOW LONG IS IT?

HOW HEAVY IS IT?

WHAT COLOUR IS IT?

HOW MANY TAPS HAS IT GOT?

HOW MUCH WATER DOES IT HOLD?

WHAT TIME CAN I COME AND SEE IT?

252 LITRES

TWO

187 CENTIMETRES

41 KILOGRAMS

TEN MINUTES TO FIVE

BRIGHT SCARLET WITH ORANGE SPOTS.

Can you see which answer should have gone with each question?

Luckily these days there are a few simple tricks to sort it all out:

> **Words to describe length always have "metre" in them such as centimetre.**
>
> **Words to describe weight always have "gram" in them, like kilogram.**
>
> **Words to describe amounts of liquid (or "capacity" – which is how much a container can hold) always have "litre" in them.**

As well as those three types of measurements, you always measure time using hours and minutes, and if you're describing a number of taps, you just give a number by itself. Obviously when you describe the colour of this bath, you don't use numbers at all although you might need to use sunglasses when you look at it.

Now then, let's travel back in time and try and sell the bath again. Telephones haven't been invented yet, so instead an arrow thuds into the arm of your chair with a note asking about the bath. You scribble out the answers on a piece of parchment and tie it to a pigeon and throw it out of the window.

Unfortunately you get everything muddled again:

How long is it?

NONE – YOU BRING WATER IN A BIG JUG.

How heavy is it?

BROWN WITH SOME SUSPICIOUS EVEN DARKER BROWN BITS.

What colour is it?

1 YARD, O FEET AND 6 INCHES.

How many taps has it got?

147 QUARTS, 1 PINT AND 18 FLUID OUNCES.

How much water does it hold?

TEN MINUTES TO FIVE.

PHEW! I'M POOPED!

What time can I come and see it?

4 STONE, 11 POUNDS AND 13 OUNCES.

Sorting out the answers is a bit tougher, isn't it? The answers about the taps and the colour are obvious enough, and the time answer is also obvious because people have used hours and minutes for hundreds of years. However the other three answers are all examples of how things were measured in the OLD DAYS – and they could make maths very murderous indeed!

Let's take a dive even further back into history...

33

Of course you know the rest – David the shepherd-boy decked Goliath with a stone from his sling and became King of Israel.

YOU'RE LUCKY HE'S IN A GOOD MOOD!

The interesting bit is – how big was Goliath?

In ancient times, the trick people used to measure things was to base everything on the human body.

- A **cubit** was the distance along the forearm from the elbow to the end of the middle finger.

- A **span** was the maximum distance that can be reached between the thumb and little finger of a wide open hand – and two spans equalled a cubit. (You can test this on your own hand and arm.)

- A **palm** was the width of a hand.

- A **digit** was the width of a finger – there were four digits in a palm and 24 digits in a cubit.

1 CUBIT

1 SPAN

1 PALM

1 DIGIT

BUT WE STILL DON'T KNOW, HOW BIG WAS GOLIATH?

Have you worked out where cubits, spans and the rest all go wrong? Of course – it's because people are different sizes. Even though the measurements were based on an adult, there are big and small adults so a cubit could be anything from 40–50 cm long. This means Goliath (at 6 cubits and 1 span) could have been as big as 3 m 25 cm high, or as small as 2 m 60 cm. Mind you, even if he was only 2 m 60 cm he was still a big lad. (If you are an OLD person and don't know about metres and other groovy metric stuff, Goliath works out to be at least 8 feet 6 inches tall. If you are a VERY OLD person then maybe you met him.)

Obviously people had to think of a better set of measurements, and for hundreds of years the "imperial" system was used. This included a measurement called a "foot". You'll be amazed to learn that this was based on the length of … a foot. (They weren't very sophisticated in those days.)

Of course this could still have gone wrong…

I'M SIX FEET TALL!

BUT I'M ONLY TWO FEET TALL!

To save confusion, the foot became standardized so that it was the same length for anybody who used it. To measure shorter things, the foot was divided into twelve little bits called "inches". (It would have made more sense if the foot had been divided into five little bits called "toes" wouldn't it? Sadly they didn't think of that.)

Because the foot was quite short, people used to measure long things such as a football pitch using "paces". Each pace was the size of a normal step and it was a convenient way of measuring distances.

Of course paces were also very approximate, so they were gradually replaced by "yards". A yard is equal to three feet (which for most adults is about the length of a long step) which is nice and simple – just as long as you don't confuse it with the *megalithic yard*.

Don't worry, you're not likely to have ever come across megalithic yards unless you're more than 4,000 years old. Experts have been examining ancient sites built by Stone Age people, and in particular they think that Stonehenge was built using a fixed unit of measure to which they've given this fancy name. A megalithic yard is slightly shorter than the standard yard – but, as Stone Age people were shorter than we are, this could tie in with the fact that they also measured things in paces!

When the Romans went roaming

If you wanted to measure the distance between two towns, feet and yards are far too short to be convenient, so the ancient Romans sorted this out by using "miles". The trouble is that a Roman mile was the length of 1,000 Roman paces, and just to make things more confusing the Romans counted TWO steps as one pace.

HOW TO MEASURE A ROMAN PACE:
- Wear ONE stiletto shoe on your right foot.
- Walk along a wet beach.
- Ignore the funny looks you get.
- The spaces between the little holes in the sand are one Roman pace long.

Thanks to the Romans travelling all over the place and beating everybody up, most of Europe got measured out in miles and so the mile was a standard length which everybody had got used to and wanted to use. Consequently when people were measuring long distances they had two choices:

- either they could make measurements by walking along wearing one stiletto shoe and dividing by 1,000;
- or they had to work out how many yards there were in a mile so they could measure it properly.

HERE COME TWO BITS OF BAD NEWS:
1 Sadly they were all a bit boring so they decided not to walk round wearing one stiletto shoe.
2 They worked out there are 1,760 yards in a mile. 1,760 – what an ugly number, eh?
Let's sum up the imperial system so far:

- 12 inches in a foot
- 3 feet in a yard
- 1,760 yards (or 5,280 feet) in a mile

Actually, it's even more murderous than that... When measuring things like fields and race courses people found yards too small and miles too big, so they gave names for other lengths in between. They had...

- $5\frac{1}{2}$ yards in a "rod" (which can also be called a "pole" or a "perch")
- 4 rods, poles or perches in a "chain"
- 10 chains in a "furlong"
- 8 furlongs in a mile

Surely it can't get worse than that?
Yes it can.
The list above uses the more common length of chain which was "Gunter's chain". This was 22 yards long – or 66 feet. Of course if you wanted to be REALLY confusing, you would use the "Engineer's chain" which was 100 feet long.

Gunter's chain was also used as the basis for measuring area. If you had a field 1 chain long by 10 chains wide, this size was called an acre. If you work it out, this comes to 4,840 square yards. (Square yards and metres get explained more on page 95.) Of course the field doesn't have to be this shape, but as long as it is 4,840 square yards in total, it is still an acre in size…

- unless you were in SCOTLAND, because in the old days a Scottish acre was 6,150 square yards (and a Scottish mile used to be 1,976 yards).
- or you were in IRELAND, because an Irish acre was 7,840 square yards (and an Irish mile used to be 2,240 yards).

Never mind, that's all you need to know – oh, unless of course you're going to sea.

The depth of water is measured in fathoms – which are 6 feet long. Of course, 120 fathoms make a "cable", and just for fun when you're sailing the ocean, instead of normal miles you use the slightly longer "nautical miles" which are 6,080 feet long

and there are three nautical miles in a "league".
Good grief – it's time we had a joke don't you think?

OK, the joke wasn't that funny, but it was better than
nothing. Anyway, can you imagine having to learn all
these different numbers at school? Not only that, but
when you had to do sums, there weren't any
calculators, so you had to learn to multiply and divide
with numbers like 1,760. Luckily for us, there were
some people who weren't too happy about this...

So much for measuring distances, but what about
weights? In the old days the main ones were in
ounces (oz), pounds (lb), stones (st), hundredweights
(cwt), and tons (T). There used to be:
- 16 oz in 1 lb, and 14 lb in 1 st
- 100 lb in a short cwt (used in America)
- 112 lb in a long cwt
- 20 cwt (which is 2,240 lbs) in a ton

41

Of course, that's only if you're talking about the most widely used AVOIRDUPOIS system.

For weighing precious stones and metals you would use the TROY system which had:

- 24 grains in a pennyweight (dwt)
- 20 pennyweights in a Troy ounce (ozt)
- 12 Troy ounces in 1 Troy pound (lbt)

The Troy system was based on a neat little coin called the silver penny which weighed exactly one pennyweight. One grain was also reckoned to be the weight of a single grain of corn.

Of course not, that would have been far too easy. In fact it was a little bit heavier, but there again the normal pound was heavier than the Troy pound because it had 16 ounces instead of 12.

As well as weights and lengths, the Imperial Standards people wanted to measure "capacity" – or in other words volumes of liquids – and so they invented a special way to do it.

A splash of inspiration

So even though one fluid ounce of water weighed one ounce in weight, everybody was still stuck with even more funny numbers. Mind you, the important thing is that a fluid ounce was a measurement of capacity, not weight. If you had a fluid ounce of mercury (which is a lot heavier than water) it would be the same size as the fluid ounce of water, but it would weigh a lot more.

Farmers used these capacity measures for buying and selling corn, but as gallons were a bit small, they used a "peck" which was 2 gallons of grain, and a "bushel" which was 4 pecks.

It was all extremely confusing, and although nearly all these strange words and measurements were in use up until the 1970s, it was about 300 years ago that the marvellous "metric" system was invented.

A good reason for liking the French
Yes, you've got to hand it to them, it was in France that the metric system was developed which made sums far simpler for everyone the whole world over.

First of all they had to choose how long a metre should be so they decided that, obviously, it should be one ten millionth of the distance from the equator to the North Pole on a line passing through Paris.

When they had worked out how long that was, they made two marks on a special metal bar exactly one metre apart and that distance started to be used as the basis for measurements all over the world. (Sadly two lines on a metal bar kept in Paris was far too nice and simple for some people, so in 1983 they got fussier and decided instead that one metre was the distance travelled by light passing through a vacuum in $\frac{1}{299,792,458}$ of a second. You wouldn't notice the difference in length, so why did they want a new system? Because it's an absolute pig to measure and you need tons and tons of posh equipment, which is just the sort of thing politicians like to insist on because they think it makes them look clever.)

Of course metres were too long to measure some things and too short to measure others but rather than make up lots of silly names, they developed a crafty scheme which just multiplied and divided by tens, hundreds and thousands – which is dead easy compared to using numbers like $5\frac{1}{2}$, 22, or 1,760.

Here's a few common examples of how this works:

To make your metre measurements 1,000 times bigger, write "kilo" in front of them. e.g. 1,000 metres is one **kilo**metre, or 1 km.

To make your metre measurements 100 times smaller, write "centi" in front of them. e.g. $\frac{1}{100}$ of a metre is one **centi**metre, or 1 cm.

To make your metre measurements 1,000 times smaller, write "milli" in front of them. e.g. $\frac{1}{1000}$ of a metre is one **milli**metre, or 1 mm.

It's simple to get used to, and these days you see "kilo", "centi" and "milli" things all over the place, not just metres. There are also lots of other less common words to describe other sizes of measurement.

If you want to measure really tiny things like germs or atoms, then these come in handy:

- **µm** is a **micro**metre (or a "micron"): $\frac{1}{1,000,000}$ ("one millionth") of a metre.
- **nm** is a **nano**metre: $\frac{1}{1,000,000,000}$ ("one thousand millionth") of a metre.
- **pm** is a **pico**metre: $\frac{1}{1,000,000,000,000}$ ("one million millionth") of a metre.
- **fm** is a **femto**metre: $\frac{1}{1,000,000,000,000,000}$ ("one thousand million millionth") of a metre.
- **am** is an **atto**metre: $\frac{1}{1,000,000,000,000,000,000}$ ("teeny weeny peeny") of a metre.

Just to give you an idea as to how small these measurements go, a single human hair is about 100 µm (or 100 microns) thick.

So much for the small stuff. If you want to measure big things like stars or galaxies, here's some of the markings you might expect on your tape measure:

- **Mm** is a **mega**metre: 1,000,000 ("one million") metres.
- **Gm** is a **giga**metre: 1,000,000,000 ("one thousand million") metres.
- **Tm** is a **tera**metre: 1,000,000,000,000 ("one million million") metres.
- **Pm** is a **peta**metre: 1,000,000,000,000,000 ("one thousand million million") metres.
- **Em** is an **exa**metre: 1,000,000,000,000,000,000 ("one million million million") metres.

The sun is about 150 gigametres away, so if anybody puts your name down to run in the 100 *exametre* event at sports day, you'd be strongly advised to get a sick note. By the way, make sure you don't mix up mm (millimetres) with Mm (megametres) because they are very different!

All these funny little names that get tagged on the front (such as nano, micro, kilo and so on) can be used for anything. If a computer has just one megabyte of memory, then it has one million bytes. If it has one gigabyte of memory, then it has one thousand million bytes. Be warned though, if it has one picobyte of memory, then you'd be better off trying to surf the net with a tub of vanilla ice-cream.

(Actually a one megabyte computer doesn't have exactly one million bytes because computers are slightly different. Everything to do with computer memory is in powers of 2, and so it turns out that one megabyte is actually 2^{20} bytes which works out to be 1,048,576 bytes. In the same way one gigabyte is really 2^{30} or 1,073,741,824 bytes. Because these powers of two just happen to work out to be close to 1,000,000 and 1,000,000,000 they use words like megabytes and gigabytes for convenience. The good bit about this is that computers are always slightly cleverer than they say they are.)

When they came to deciding how big litres should be, they set up this cunning wheeze:

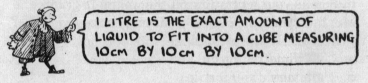

I LITRE IS THE EXACT AMOUNT OF LIQUID TO FIT INTO A CUBE MEASURING 10cm BY 10cm BY 10cm.

For smaller amounts they used millilitres for measuring, and for larger amounts they *could* have used kilolitres – but as a kilolitre is the exact amount that fits into a cube measuring $1 \text{ m} \times 1 \text{ m} \times 1 \text{ m}$, they generally used cubic metres instead.

When it came to measuring weight they devised an equally helpful trick and said that:

A LITTLE CUBE OF WATER MEASURING I cm BY I cm BY I cm WEIGHS EXACTLY I GRAM.

If you work it out, you'll find it takes 1,000 of these little cubes to make a litre, so a one litre of water weighs 1,000 grams which is one kilogram.

If you have a cubic metre of water (i.e. enough water to fill a tank measuring 1 m × 1 m × 1 m) this will weigh 1,000 kilograms – which is one metric tonne. (This is roughly the same weight as 15 adults.)

Even now people are still changing over from imperial to metric measures. Quite often on packets of food in supermarkets you get the weight in grams and also in pounds and ounces – but how do they compare?

Here are a few examples:

- 1 metre is 1·1 yards
- 1 kilometre is 0·6 miles
- 1 kilogram is 2·2 pounds
- 1 litre is 1·75 pints
  and best of all...
- 1 tonne is 1 ton!

First you have to convert the 5 oz to lbs – and as there are 16 oz in 1 lb you get $\frac{5}{16}$ lbs. You then divide this by 2·2 which gives you 0·142 kg or 142 g.

Actually these conversions aren't EXACTLY correct, for instance 1 litre is really 1·76056 pints, but we don't want to make murderous maths even more murderous than absolutely necessary, do we?

All change in Britain
Obviously multiplying everything by tens and hundreds is simple, and most countries have their money based on this. There are 100 cents to the dollar, 100 cents to the Euro, 100 gziphs to the fwoj and so on.

In Britain there are 100 pence to the pound, but that only started on 15 February 1971. Before that there were 4 farthings to a penny, 12 pennies to a shilling, and 20 shillings to the pound! Everybody got well confused when it all changed over because shillings suddenly became 5p and even worse, 2·4 old pennies were worth one new penny.

There were also other odd amounts. A "groat" was 4 pennies, a "florin" was 2 shillings, a "crown" was 5 shillings and a "guinea" was 21 shillings – which was just over £1. Quite often you had a mixture of coins in your pocket that included "half a crown" coins that were worth $12\frac{1}{2}$p, and also "florins" that were worth 10p!

So next time you think that sums involving measurements or money are too murderous – spare a thought for all the old people you know who didn't have the marvellous metric system!

Does everybody use the metric system?
Not quite. Even though the metric system is neat and convenient, some of the old measures are still in

use. Nearly everybody in the United Kingdom and America still describes distances in miles and speed in miles per hour. Also lots of older people still think in yards, feet and inches because they had to work so hard at school to understand it, they can't get it out of their heads. Pounds (in weight) and pints are also common.

There is an important point to note here. Whatever units you are using, you must make it clear. Don't just assume that everybody is working in metric units because the consequences could be murderous!

Imagine you spent years of work and billions of pounds on developing a rocket to go to Mars. Once you've got everything ready you then have to wait for a day when Mars is in the right place, the weather is reasonable and everything is set to go so that at last you can blast your rocket off.

The trip takes nine whole months during which the rocket travels over 650 million kilometres, so you can imagine the relief you feel as the rocket safely approaches the planet. All it needs now are a few minor course corrections to make sure the rocket orbits properly, so you quickly zap these across space before the rocket flies round to the back of the planet where your radio telescopes can't track it.

At long last you know all your cash and effort will be repaid by the stream of priceless information about Mars, but before the rocket can transmit anything back to you it has to emerge from the back of the planet. All you can do in the meantime is sit and wait ... and wait ... and wait ... and start to panic a bit ... and wait ... and start panicking a lot ... and wait...

This is a true story. The rocket disappeared in September 1999 so it's lucky that nobody was on it! But what happened? It turns out that the rocket was programmed to expect its instructions in metres and kilograms, but the people that made the rocket gave the instructions for the final course corrections in feet and pounds. What a murderous mistake!

So why do horses need hands?
There are some traditional activities that refuse to compromise with metric, and people with horses are a good example. Although human runners compete in events like the 10,000 metres or the 80 metre hurdles, in Britain horses tend to run distances measured in old lengths such as 5 furlongs, or 1 mile 6 furlongs. The size of a horse is also judged in "hands".

A hand is the width of an adult hand at the widest point, and is about 4 inches or 10 centimetres.

The size of a horse is measured from the ground to the top of the shoulder – and to be a horse you need to be at least $14\frac{1}{2}$ hands high – otherwise you're a pony!

A final footnote

Unfortunately the metric system isn't all joy because as the old imperial measures die out, so do some fine old jokes. How about these:

Or even:

After many years of faithful service, this could be the last book that these top gags ever appear in. Sad, isn't it?

METRES FOR EVERYTHING

Any time that you're measuring lengths or distances, you can always choose whether you use kilometres, metres, centimetres or millimetres and so on. However if you need to mix measurements together it is much easier just to use plain metres. It saves a lot of confusion and having to write km or mm or just m after every measurement. It's also a fact that most science boffins have appalling handwriting, and it could be hard to tell if they've written "m" or "mm" or even "mummy" for that matter.

As we've seen before, if we only allow ourselves to use one sort of unit, we could end up using tons of zeros but there's a sneaky way of avoiding this. First of all let's see how to deal with a really big measurement. Anybody got one?

Oh look, it's the evil Gollarks from the planet Zog who've come to invade us.

Yeah we guessed that, but how far have you come?

Brilliant! That's just what we need.

Yeah yeah, whatever. Now let's look at this distance of yours and, if you don't mind, the first thing we'll do is just use three significant digits. That makes it into 483,000,000,000,000,000,000 km.

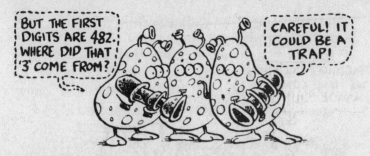

Stop whispering, it's very rude. Now what we'll do is put a decimal point after the first digit so we get 4·83.

Don't get your ear-stalks knotted. Now we count up how many places we would need to move the decimal point along to turn 4·83 into 483,000,000,000,000,000,000 and the answer is twenty places. Another way of looking at it is to say that you have travelled 4·83 × 100,000,000,000,000,000,000 km.

Of course that's in kilometres but we want to work in metres, so we'll put three extra zeros on the end of the long number because there's a thousand metres in a kilometre, you see. That gives us 100,000,000,000,000,000,000,000. Now here comes the good bit: this number is the same as 10^{23}.

NO IT ISN'T

Yes it is. Don't you know about *powers of ten*? It's dead simple because powers are little numbers that appear in the top corner after a number, for instance 10^2 is "ten to the power of two" and is the same as two tens multiplied together. Of course $10 \times 10 = 100$ and so $10^2 = 100$. You can use powers other than 2, for instance 10^6 is six tens multiplied together which is $10 \times 10 \times 10 \times 10 \times 10 \times 10$, and this comes to 1,000,000 which you'll notice is a one with six zeros after it. That's why 10^{23} is the same as a "1" with 23 zeros after it.

Instead of writing your distance as 482,675,578,901,775,330,024 km, we can write it as 4.83×10^{23} m.

ENOUGH, EARTHLINGS! WE'RE GOING TO SET THIS ANTI-NEUTRON DESTROYER TO WIPE OUT YOUR ENTIRE SOLAR SYSTEM!

AND IN THE MEANTIME, OVER GOES YOUR FIRST WASTE BIN!

STOUFF

Oh dear! They got themselves into a bit of a mood, didn't they? Now you're probably thinking it's time to put a handkerchief over your head or hide behind the sofa or something, but in fact the Gollarks have made a tiny but crucial mistake...

Did you see what they did wrong?

If you look carefully at the zzaps setting you'll see it reads 8.91×10^{-14}. Now to be honest, if it said 10^{14} then we might have been in BIG trouble, but there's a teeny little minus sign just before the "14". That little minus sign has just saved Earth!

If the setting had been 8.91×10^{14} then that would have meant a power of 891,000,000,000,000 zzaps. (To work it out you move the decimal point 14 places to the right and fill up the empty places with zeros.) That's a lot of zzaps, but fortunately it wasn't 10^{14} it was 10^{-14}. The little minus means that you move the decimal point *the other way*!

To work out 8.91×10^{-14} you move the decimal point 14 places to the *left*. That way we were only hit with 0.0000000000000891 of a zzap.

So, as you can see, with this system you can give measurements in metres for the most massive things and also for the very tiniest without writing out loads and loads of numbers. This also explains why one Angstrom can be written as 10^{-10} m. We know an Angstrom is 0.0000000001 m, and with this system it becomes 1.00×10^{-10} but obviously you don't need to put the 1.00 in because anything multiplied by 1 stays the same.

(DECIMALS HINT: When you're converting a number like $3 \cdot 75 \times 10^{-5}$ into a decimal, you subtract one from the little number above the ten, and that's how many zeros you put in after the decimal point. With $3 \cdot 75 \times 10^{-5}$ you just take 1 from the 5 which means you just put in four zeros and it comes to $0 \cdot 0000375$. If you had $7 \cdot 34 \times 10^{-1}$ this just becomes $0 \cdot 734$.)

What do calculators make of all this?

If you've got a calculator, you might well find it uses this system automatically. Put in a massive sum so that the answer won't fit on the screen such as 334455×66778899.

Here's what you might get:

This is a pretty clever calculator. It has given you 10 significant digits, and the "E13" at the end means you multiply the number by 10^{13}.

This one is good too – the little "13" is telling you the power of ten you need.

Not bad – 8 significant digits and again it tells you to multiply by 10^{13}. (Can you see how this calculator

61

might have been a tiny bit cleverer? It should have rounded the last 6 up to a 7, because as the cleverer calculators showed us, the next digit would have been a 6 which is bigger than 5. Most calculators don't bother with rounding up, and for that matter they never take their turn at doing the dishes or tidying the bedroom either.)

This one lost the plot a bit because there's an E at the end with no numbers after it. Never mind, you should still be able to work out what power of ten is involved by doing the sum roughly. First simplify the sum by rounding the numbers off to just ONE significant digit. Yahoo! You get 300000×70000000. Then multiply the two digits together and get $3 \times 7 = 21$. Now count up all the zeros (in this case there's 12) and this tells you that your answer is about 21×10^{12}. As the calculator answer starts with the digits 22, you can see this is roughly the value of 21 that you worked out, so you put the decimal point in after the 22. Then fill in the remaining digits of the calculator answer to get $22 \cdot 334536 \times 10^{12}$. Finally, if you want to be flash, you can move the point and change the power to get the more usual looking $2 \cdot 2334536 \times 10^{13}$.

This one also lost the plot, and even worse it had a guess where the point should go. You've got to admire its spirit, but that E by itself tells you to ignore any decimal points. (Sometimes they get so confused they show more than one!) You can still have a go at the correct answer using the method above.

If you get an "E" on the display by itself, then at least the calculator's being honest. It hasn't a clue what the answer is and is feeling a little bit shy and might break into tears at any moment. It just wants to be left alone in the bottom of a handbag next to the tissues and an old lipstick.

This calculator has an attitude problem. It realizes that you didn't really want to calculate 334455×66778899, you were just messing about. Mind you, that shouldn't make any difference, so if a calculator won't do what it's told, then wire it up to the output terminals of a giant nuclear power station. That'll teach the stroppy little box who's boss.

BIG THINGS, TRUNDLES AND THE TEN-TONNE RULER

What happens if the thing you want to measure is longer than your ruler or tape?

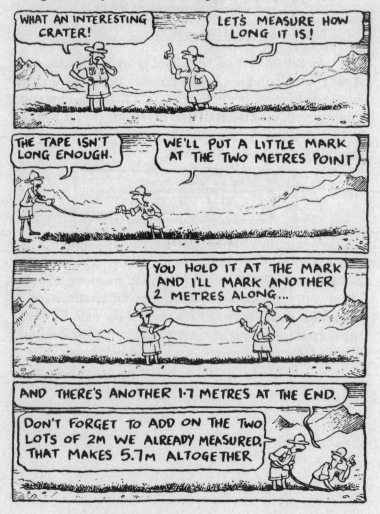

Measuring very tall things

This is such a neat trick that by law it has to appear in any book about measuring otherwise the publishers get busted and the police confiscate their lemonade supply and draw goofy teeth on all the posters of pop stars that are stuck over everybody's desks.

THE PROBLEM:

There's a great big tall flagpole sticking out of the ground and you need to measure the height, and you don't fancy climbing up the side with your ruler measuring it bit by bit.

THE SOLUTION:

The main part of the trick is to stick a stick in the ground and wait for the sun to come out. Isn't that just completely brilliant?

There is a bit more… If you can be bothered to wait, then the easy way is to wait until the length of the stick's shadow is exactly the same as the height of the stick. When this happens, then you know that the shadow of the flagpole will be the same as its height!

If you think about it, it's obvious how this works. Suppose your stick is 1 m high, then the shadow will be 1 m long. If your stick is 2 m high, then the shadow will be 2 m long. If your stick is as high as the flagpole, then the length of the shadow is the same as this height. However you don't need a stick as high as the flagpole, you just measure the flagpole's shadow!

AND IF YOU CAN'T WAIT...
Sadly there are times when this doesn't work, usually because you can't be bothered to wait until the stick's shadow is the same as the stick's height. Another reason might be that there isn't enough flat ground for the full length flagpole's shadow to fall on and so you need to take a measurement when the sun is higher and shadows are shorter. In this case you'll have to do a simple sum but first you need to stick your stick in and measure the following:

Make sure the lengths are all in the same units – if in doubt use metres! Now then, here come the sums:
- Divide the height of the stick by the length of the stick's shadow.
- Take this answer and multiply it by length of the flagpole's shadow.
- That's it!

If you prefer formulas, then it looks like this:

$$\text{Flagpole height} = \frac{\text{stick height}}{\text{stick shadow length}} \times \text{flagpole shadow length}$$

(If a formula has two numbers with a line dividing them, it means the number on the top is being divided by the number on the bottom.)

Other tall things
This brilliant trick doesn't just work for flagpoles, it's also good for thin trees, basketball players and trains that are parked standing upright rather than with all their wheels on the track. (This saves a lot of space in railway yards.) It is also the same trick that Thag used to rescue the princess from the tower in *Murderous Maths*.

However the trick does not work so well for wide trees or buildings with a sloping or domed roof, but you can still make a good estimation. All you need is a friend called Bertie.
- Measure how tall Bertie is.
- Get Bertie to stand by the building.
- Stand back a long way.

67

- Imagine a pile of Berties all standing on each other's heads going up to the top of the building.
- Multiply the number of imaginary Berties by his height – and there's your answer!

BINGO! You have performed a miracle of measurement that would have been murderous to work out if you didn't know the secret!

Bent things

A lot of times when you are measuring length, it isn't in a straight line. For instance, if you think your head has grown to make space for the extra brains you've developed from reading this book, you need to measure the distance around it. Obviously a ruler isn't much use, but if you put a tape measure round your head you can read off the result.

If you don't have a tape measure, then you can use a piece of string and make a mark where the distance comes to on the string. You then pull the string out straight and hold it against a ruler.

Sometimes you have to measure wiggly lines such as roads on maps. One way to do this is to get your string again and very carefully lay it along the line and then check it against a ruler. The other way is to use a trundle wheel.

HOW TO MAKE A TRUNDLE WHEEL
You will need:
- some nice stiff card
- a pointed stick (an old pencil is perfect for this)
- a drawing pin
- a 4,000 watt surgical laser cutter with digital calibration, caesium emission neutralizers and dynamic heat shields. (If you haven't got one handy then a pair of scissors will do.)

What you do:
First you need to cut a circle out of the card. This circle should be 63·7 mm across, which by a happy chance is exactly this size:

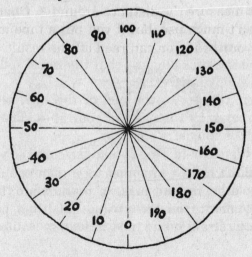

- This is your "wheel" and the next thing is to draw little lines around the edge that are 10 mm apart and number them. If your wheel is exactly the right size you should have room for exactly 20 lines. (Actually you'll have 0·19452 mm spare but that's far too small to worry about.)
- You then pin the wheel to the stick so that the point doesn't quite go over the edge.

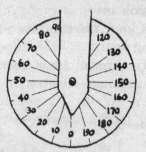

You're now ready to measure your wiggly line!
- Set the wheel so that the "0" is by the point of the stick.
- Hold the stick upright and put the edge of the wheel on the start of the wiggly line you're measuring.
- Move the stick along so that the wheel rolls along the wiggly line.
- When you get to the end of the line, see what number is by the point of your stick. That's how long the line is!

Two things to note. One is to make sure the wheel is turning the right way round as you move the stick. And the other is that if it goes round more than one complete turn, you have to add 200 mm for each complete revolution on to your final measurement.

How to use a ten-tonne ruler

Normally when you use a ruler you can just pick it up and plonk it alongside the line you want to measure, then read off the answer. All nice and simple, but what happens if you can't put the ruler where you need it?

Quite often you'll come across rulers that are not on a long strip of plastic, instead they might be printed in a book or on a map. Another common problem is that your ruler is glued to the side of a desk or drawing board. A very unusual problem is that your ruler is made out of reinforced concrete and weighs ten tonnes – so what do you do?

HELP! I'VE DROPPED MY RULER!

One answer is to use a piece of string as we've described before, but if the line you want to measure is straight there's a posh way of doing it.

If you've got a geometry set, you'd be forgiven for thinking that it is full of diabolical weapons. There's an assortment of flat plastic bits that you can flick for miles, there will be at least one thing with a really sharp metal spike sticking out of the end and there might even be a gadget with two metal spikes hinged together which is called a "pair of dividers".

HMMM

Dividers have several uses:
- Getting seafood out of shells.
- Pinning photos on the wall.
- Doing experiments on insects.
- Helping yourself to a double amount of cocktail sausages at parties.
- Working out the area of beautifully polished tables (but this is not recommended as you'll find out later).
- Pushing grapes and elephants under water. (Highly recommended as you'll see later. Gosh, this book is packed with good stuff isn't it?)
- Measuring straight lines the posh way.

If you want to be really cool when measuring a straight line, what you do is open up the dividers so that the two points go exactly on the ends of the line. You then move the dividers over to your ruler (being very careful not to open or close them at all) and put one point on the "0". Of course the other point will then indicate the exact measurement. This might all seem a bit fancy, but using this method shows the world that you are simply dripping in sheer class – and better still it means that if you're stuck with a ten-tonne ruler, you can use it.

HOW MANY METRES ARE THERE ON THE HEAD OF A PIN?

Not many, you might say, and who could blame you? Metres are long things and pinheads are only tiny, so you might imagine you could only get about 0·001 of a metre on one. Have a look:

°

There, hasn't Mr Reeve made a neat job of drawing the pinhead? However, we do realize that there are one or two Murderous Maths readers who might not be able to make out all the exquisite details, so here the picture has been enlarged for you:

As you can see, the line of 1 mm just about fits across with a tiny bit to spare. That seems to answer the question, apart from one niggling little doubt – could Mr Reeve fit a second line on?

Yes! So that means we can get 2 mm on to our pinhead and possibly more. Of course there's no reason why the lines have to be straight either, so let's see if we can get a longer wiggly line onto the pinhead.

THIS LINE IS ABOUT 12 mm.

As you can see, if you really try to fill the space up then the line can be a lot longer. And if the line is thinner – it could be even longer still.

 THIS LINE IS ABOUT 70 mm.

It's no good, this will need enlarging a bit more.

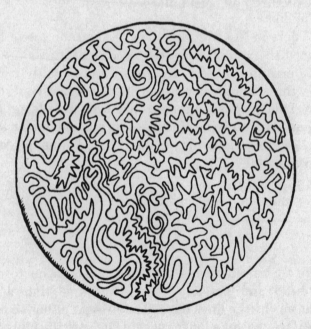

VERY IMPORTANT THING TO DO

Before reading any more, there's a completely VITAL task for you to complete. Don't even think about continuing this book until you've found the two ends of the line in the picture. Remember, one end is not good enough. Even the Evil Reeve with all his accursed powers of draughtsmanship cannot draw a one-ended line, so be sure to find them both.

Now that we've got that out of our systems, let's get to the two vital points about this lines on pinhead stuff:

● If you make the line thinner, then you can make it longer and still have room to fit it on the pinhead.

● There is NO LIMIT to how thin a line can be.

Here's the really scary bit. You could draw a line long enough to reach the moon and back, but if it was thin enough it would still fit on the head of a pin! This is because **a real line only has length** – it has absolutely no thickness at all. The fancy way of describing this is to say that a line is "one dimensional".

In the olden days when maths was first being invented, they decided that a straight line was the shortest distance between two points. This makes sense if you think about it. Look at these two dots, how far apart are they?

The straight line is 50 mm long, and obviously that's how far the dots are apart. The wiggly line is a lot longer but even though it joins the dots up it's got nothing to do with how far apart they are. The other thing to notice here is that it wouldn't matter if you joined the dots with a thick line or a thin line, the two dots are still the same distance apart and that's the only measurement we're concerned with. As we said before: lines only have length.

What confuses everything is that when we try to mark lines on paper we have to give them a little bit of thickness (which is usually called "width") otherwise nobody would be able to see them. This width might only be tiny, but it means that we haven't drawn a true line, what we've got is a coloured-in *area*. Although a real line would not take up any space on the page, areas always do. When it comes to measurements, **an area has length and width**, or if you prefer, an area is "two dimensional". (If you want to know all the freaky dimensional stuff, it's explained in *More Murderous Maths*.)

So the answer to "How many metres are there on the head of a pin?" is "As many as you like!"

How to put a real line on this page

Would you like to put a line on this page that only has length but no width at all? It might seem impossible but the trick is that you don't use a pencil or pen, you use scissors.

DON'T YOU DARE CUT THIS BOOK OR I SHALL LOSE MY TEMPER!

He's right, you shouldn't cut books, but just suppose you were to do one very neat cut from the edge of the page between these two drawn lines.

When you hold the page down flat, you'll just be able to make out the very thin line where the cut is – and yet it has no width! You will have made a perfect one-dimensional line.

Have you done a cut? Quickly, put the scissors away and let's hope nobody gets hurt. Now turn the page over.

Oh dear, look down there! When you saw this book was called *Murderous Maths*, it never dawned on you how murderous it could be did it? Well, let that be an important lesson to you, never ever cut pages in books.

Quick! Change your clothes, put on a false beard, grab a fake passport and hurry away to the safety of the next chapter...

THE SEALED BOX PROBLEM

You have to be alert at all times, don't you? Even when you are popping out to the shops to get an emergency box of washing powder, you should always check that there are no unexplained sensor pads in the pavement – and certainly you should never accidentally step on one. Still, that's what you did, and therefore it's no wonder that two metal clamps suddenly shot out of a nearby dustbin and grabbed your legs as the whole section of street you were on flipped right over.

That's why you are now dangling upside down from a dustbin attached to the ceiling of a secret underground cavern. You watch amazed as little bits of dust and litter detach themselves from what was the street and float down to the floor below your head. Oh boy – it doesn't take a lot of imagination to work out who's behind this, and sure enough you hear a familiar voice...

"Har har! Thanks for *dropping* in."

Yes, it's your arch-enemy Professor Fiendish and, my, doesn't he look pleased with himself, in an upside-down sort of way.

"I've really got you this time," he gloats. "Be honest, what do you think of my brilliant trap?"

"As predictable as ever," you say with a bored yawn.

"Predictable?" gasps the professor. "It's awesome! Do you know how long it took me to tunnel under the road, and then build a complete replica piece of street and attach it to the underside of the real street so that when it swivels over nobody will notice the difference?"

"One hour, twenty-three minutes and fourteen seconds."

"Eh?" gasped the professor. "What makes you think it took one hour, twenty-three…"

But then the professor notices that you are giving him a rather pitiful stare.

"Oh I see. That's a sort of sarcastic joke, is it? Well tee hee, and for your information it's taken me years! Every tiny detail had to be meticulously planned, every technical component was checked and double-checked, it's fantastic!"

"Yeah yeah, now let me down!"

You wriggle yourself free of the clamps, but in doing so you knock the lid off the dustbin. You can't help smirking as a mass of old fish skins, soggy tea bags, cold beans and potato peelings lands on his head.

"I'm glad every tiny detail was planned," you say as you land lightly on your feet next to him.

The professor looks up at the dustbin in fury. PLOP! A smelly nappy finally unsticks itself from the bottom of the bin, and hits him square on the kisser.

"Ho ho!" you laugh jollily. "Well done, Fiendish. You're right, it's fantastic! Still, if you don't mind, I must be getting home to avert a whiffy sock crisis."

Clutching your box of washing powder, you head for the door.

"Not so fast!" says the professor. "You don't leave until you've solved my most diabolical challenge yet! And that may be NEVER!"

You try to look unconcerned, but there's a particularly nasty glint in his eye. There might even be a nasty glint in the other eye too, but you can't really tell because the nappy is stuck to it.

"You will stay here until you've solved the Sealed Box Problem!" he snarls.

"What box is that then?" you ask.

"Any sealed box will do," says the professor. "Even that box of washing powder. To solve the problem, all you have to do is tell me what is the length of the longest stick you could fit into that box."

You look at the box and realize that obviously the longest stick you could fit in would go from one top corner, down through the very centre of the box to the furthest bottom corner. In other words, it is the longest diagonal of the box.

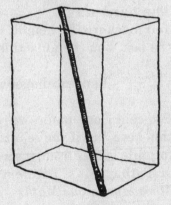

"Here's a ruler to help you measure the distance," says the professor. "And when you get the answer, tap the numbers into the control panel on the wall and you will be released."

"But I can't measure the distance without opening the box!" you say.

"I know!" says the professor. "They don't call me Fiendish for nothing! Har har!"

And so as he goes for a shower, you're left wondering how you can measure the inside of the box without opening it!

This is a classic old problem and there are two ways of getting the answer...

The hard way
You measure the height, the width and the depth of the box. You then use this formula:

$$\text{Longest diagonal} = \sqrt{h^2 + w^2 + d^2}$$

Poo-eeh! Don't panic, we're not going to worry about this here, but if you're interested to know where this formula comes from, it's a three-dimensional version of Pythagoras's Theorem – which is explained in *More Murderous Maths*.

The trouble with this formula is that the professor didn't leave you a calculator to work out the squares and square roots, but with a bit of ingenuity you might realize there's a far simpler solution to this measuring problem!

Have you realized it yet? If so then bend your mouth round to your cheek to give yourself a big kiss, and then you can escape and get home to the washing machine. If you haven't realized it … well never mind. It's the sort of problem you need to have bubbling away in the back of your mind for a while and then suddenly you hit on the answer. So we'll let you have a think about it for a bit.

Let's just hope the answer doesn't occur anywhere embarrassing.

Have you had a think? Then turn over and see how your idea compares to this one...

The easy solution

This is a lot easier than a pile of maths! Here's what you do:

- Stand the box on a flat surface and mark where the four bottom corners are. To make these instructions clear we'll call these four corner marks A, B, C and D.

- Move the box over as if you were standing it next to its original position. The corners that were on A and B will now be on marks C and D.

- All you do is measure the distance from mark A to the corner of the box that is above mark C. There's your answer!

84

You tap the numbers into the control panel and immediately a steel door slides aside revealing a staircase that leads back up to reality. Just as you step through you hear footsteps scampering up from behind you.

"How did you ever arrive at the answer?" gasps the professor.

"Aha!" you explain a trifle smugly. "I created a virtual box which I could measure. It is exactly as wide, deep and high as the solid box, but I could put the ruler in it!"

"A virtual box?" he gibbers. "But my trap was foolproof!"

"Virtually foolproof," you reply as you climb the stairs into the sunlight, "but not completely foolproof."

Will he never learn? You can't defeat murderous maths.

DO YOU SHAPE UP?

This chapter has a maths test in it for which you will need to allow exactly three hours and five minutes. This is because it will take you five minutes to answer all the questions, and then three hours to get the smug grin off your face because you found it so easy. To make it even easier, here's a couple of useful descriptions to know:

PARALLEL
When two lines are parallel, this means that there is always the same distance between them, and if you drew them on for ever they would never ever touch. The rails on a straight piece of railway track have to be parallel or the train would fall off.

A RIGHT ANGLE
This is what people call a square corner such as the corner of this book. Lots of shapes depend on having one or more right angles and here's how to make your own personal set of right angles:
1 You can use any piece of paper you like.

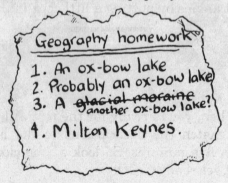

Geography homework
1. An ox-bow lake
2. Probably an ox-bow lake
3. A ~~glacial moraine~~ another ox-bow lake?
4. Milton Keynes.

2 Fold the paper in half.

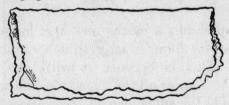

3 Fold it in half again so that the folded edges meet.

4 Open it out – and you will see four right angles in the middle!

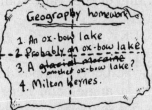

Geography homework

1. An ox-bow lake
2. ~~Probably an ox-bow lake~~
3. A ~~glacial moraine~~ another ox-bow lake?
4. Milton Keynes.

When people draw shapes, they usually indicate any right angles by putting a little box in the corner.

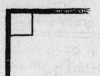

Right then, you're ready for the test. All you have to do is match the descriptions to the numbered shapes in five minutes. So look at the clock, check the time, get ready... GO!

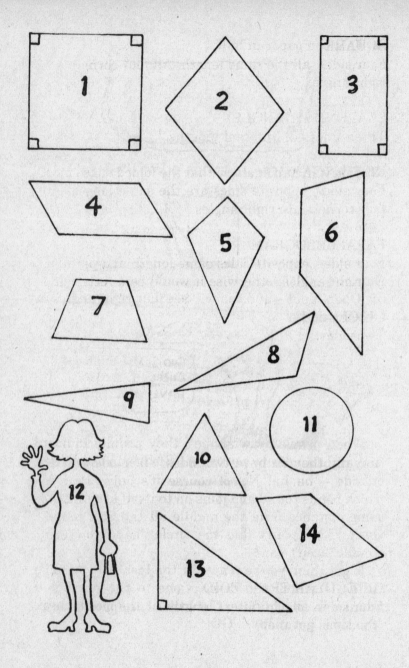

SQUARE
Four sides, all the same length. All four corners are right angles.

SCALENE TRIANGLE
Three sides, all different lengths.

RECTANGLE
Four sides, opposite sides are the same length. All four corners are right angles.

PARALLELOGRAM
Four sides, opposite sides same length and parallel. No right angles (otherwise it would be a rectangle).

CIRCLE
Two sides.

TWO SIDES? RUBBISH! CIRCLES ONLY HAVE ONE SIDE!

Actually they do have two sides: an inside and an outside – ha ha! No, of course it's only one side which bends round and joins on to itself keeping the same distance from the middle all the way round. Gosh, if you can't find the circle shape you're in trouble, aren't you?

IRREGULAR TRAPEZOID
Four sides, all of different lengths. One opposite pair of sides is parallel.

KITE
Four sides, two short sides meet and two long sides meet. Probably no right angles, but there might be one or two. Who cares? The main thing is, does it fly?

EQUILATERAL TRIANGLE
Three sides, all the same length.

RHOMBUS
Four sides all the same length. No right angles. (Otherwise it would be a square!)

THE TERRIBLY LOVELY VERONICA GUMFLOSS
Lots of sides and angles and a temper to take the stripes off a tiger.

ISOSCELES TRIANGLE
Three sides, two have the same length.

ISOSCELES TRAPEZOID
Four sides, two are parallel. The two sloping sides are the same length.

IRREGULAR QUADRILATERAL
Four sides, none parallel. At least one side must be a different length from the others. (The others can all be the same or different.)

RIGHT-ANGLED TRIANGLE
Three sides. One angle must be a right angle.
NOTE: The side opposite the right angle is always the longest and gets called the "hypotenuse". Right-angled triangles can be either isosceles or scalene.

Check your score with this table:

- 14 correct answers… You are utterly fantastically brilliant.
- 13 correct answers… You can't have counted your answers correctly.
- 0–12 correct answers… Who dropped this book into your playpen?

This test included just about every different shape you can make with three or four straight sides and if your brain needs a bit of an extra challenge you can colour them in. (Of course if you got this book out of a library then DON'T colour the shapes in. If you do, the secret library police will sneak into your room when you're out and swap all your favourite books for great big smelly old volumes with titles like "The National Register of Eggs" or "The Political Memoirs of Jefferson ffolkes-Babbington". Urgh!)

Most of these shapes don't come up very often, for instance when was the last time you stepped onto a trapezoid-shaped bath mat? It's worth knowing how to go about measuring some of the others though, so let's hit it.

91

FROM SQUARES TO CURRY STAINS

SHAPE	MEASUREMENT DIFFICULTY	TOUGHNESS OF SUMS	FORMULA
SQUARES	EASY, JUST MEASURE ONE SIDE.	UTTERLY WEEDY	a^2
RECTANGLES	EASY, MEASURE LENGTH AND WIDTH.	EAT 'EM FOR BREAKFAST	ab
RIGHT-ANGLED TRIANGLES	EASY, MEASURE TWO SHORTER SIDES.	NO WORRIES	$\frac{1}{2}hb$
OTHER TRIANGLES	ER... NEEDS SOME SKILL.	NOT TOO BAD	$\frac{1}{2}hb$
FANCY SHAPES WITH STRAIGHT EDGES	NEED BREAKING TO BITS.	EASY BUT BORING	MAKE YOUR OWN
CIRCLES	TRICKIER.	UGLY	πr^2
CURRY STAINS	NEED TO USE CUNNING METHODS.	GOOD LUCK— YOU'LL NEED IT.	????

As we found out before, an area always needs at least two measurements, although sometimes you use the same measurement twice. You also need to do a few sums, so to give you a general idea of what you're up against, here's a handy chart to show you how hard various shapes are. Each shape also has a formula which is listed here, but if you don't understand them then don't worry because they get explained properly later on.

Rectangles and squares
Let's forget about squares immediately because a square is just a rectangle which happens to have all its sides the same length. You can see rectangles all over the place such as the front of this book, doors, football pitches, bank notes, the bottoms of drawers, the sides of cornflake packets and so on. When you measure rectangles, you need to get the length and the width so let's grab something rectangular and see how we get on. We'll pop into Fogsworth Manor and see what we can find. Aha! That table looks perfect.

Thanks for being understanding.

When we measure up this table, we find it's 1·5 metres long by 1·2 metres wide. With rectangles, the usual way of writing this is to put 1·5 m × 1·2 m and suddenly it's decision time!

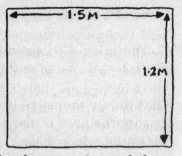

- If you wanted to describe *the exact size and shape* of the table, you would say that it is rectangular and give the measurements as 1·5 m × 1·2 m
- If you just want to measure the total *area* then you're not too worried about the actual shape. It could be really long and narrow or short and fat or it could be bent round in a curve with lumps sticking out of the side but that's not important. All you want to know is how much space there is on the tabletop, so let's see how to work it out.

So the measurements of this rectangle are 1·5 m × 1·2 m and you'll see that a times sign has mysteriously appeared in the middle. This is no accident because if we multiply the length and the width together the answer is a measurement of the area of the rectangle. Quite often people just call these two measurements "a" and "b" so you get:

Area of rectangle = length × width = a × b = ab

With formulas you don't usually bother writing "times" signs in, instead you just put the letters together. If you want the formula for the area of a square, don't forget that the length is the same as the width so you end up with:

Area of a square = a × a which gets written as a^2

Let's work out the area for the table now. We get: 1·5 × 1·2 = 1·8. Hang on though, it's 1·8 *whats?*

What do we measure area in?

Suppose the area of the tabletop was 1·8 metres – that's a bit odd because 1·8 metres is a measure of length. As we've already seen, we could fit 1·8 metres on the head of a pin if we wanted to.

HOW THE BLISTERING PANTS AM I SUPPOSED TO EAT MY DINNER OFF THE HEAD OF A PIN?

Calm down, Colonel. If you think about it, we got the area by multiplying 1·5 metres by 1·2 metres and if we ignore the numbers for a minute, that means we've multiplied metres by metres. As you may know: if you multiply anything by itself we say it's been "squared" – for example, 3 × 3 = "3 squared" which you can write as 3^2. In this case we've got metres × metres which we call "square metres" or you can even put "m^2" if you like. This means the area of your table comes to 1·8 m^2.

I DON'T CARE WHAT IT COMES TO. I WANT TO EAT MY DINNER!

COME ON COLONEL, WE'LL USE THE CORNER CUPBOARD AS A TABLE!

HINT: When you have to take more than one measurement make sure you use the same units. Suppose you said the table was 1·5 m × 1200 mm, when you work out the area you would get 1800 metremillimetres which you'll be glad to know is complete rubbish.

Different units of area

The obvious ones are:

- 1 square millimetre = 1 mm × 1 mm
- 1 square centimetre = 1 cm × 1 cm
- 1 square metre = 1 m × 1 m.

For massive areas like countries we use square kilometres, but before we get to that size there are two more common units.

For areas such as fields people might use 1 *hectare* = 100 m × 100 m (or 10,000 square metres) or they might even use old-fashioned *acres*. There are 2·47 acres in a hectare, and you might be tempted to say that's about $2\frac{1}{2}$. After all, if you're only talking about muddy old fields covered in thistles and cow poo, a difference of 0·03 of an acre hardly seems to matter does it? Actually it's about 120 square metres, which is the size of a barn, so before you say it doesn't matter, make sure that whatever's in the barn isn't going to mind.

A strange bit of maths to stop it raining

Yes – incredible as it seems – if you're stuck indoors because it's heaving down with rain, don't despair. Thanks to this Murderous Maths experiment you can discover something amazing about areas, and also you can stop it raining at the same time! That's pretty spooky, isn't it?

To harness the darker forces of maths you first need to prepare your mind by considering this question: we know there are 1,000 millimetres in 1 metre but how many square millimetres are there in a square metre? If you want to work it out with a sum, you start off by saying 1,000 mm = 1 m. Next you square both sides (which means you multiply each side by itself) and get 1,000 mm × 1,000 mm = 1 m × 1 m. This comes out as 1,000,000 mm² = 1 m² Good grief! Is this sum really telling us that there are *one million* square millimetres in one square metre? If you find this maths fact too amazing to believe, there's a simple way of checking and that's when the magic starts.

WARNING!

IT IS ADVISED THAT YOU DO NOT ATTEMPT
THIS SPELL IF IT IS YOUR BIRTHDAY IN
LESS THAN TWO WEEKS...

All you do is get a piece of paper measuring exactly 1 metre × 1 metre, then you get a very sharp pencil and divide it up into 1,000 strips each 1 millimetre wide in one direction, and then divide it up into 1,000 strips 1 millimetre wide in the other direction. In this way you will have divided the paper into lots and lots of 1 millimetre squares. Has it stopped raining yet? If not, then never mind because there's more sorcery to come.

Carefully cut out all the little squares. (If you like you can drop them into a cauldron and stir them round using a unicorn's spike while you chant some Latin words backwards, but to be honest Murderous Maths experiments are potent enough without resorting to cheap gimmicks.) Check outside. Still raining? If so, then it's time for the final wizardry...

Count the squares.

That's all there is to it. By the time you've counted them you'll see the rain has stopped. Actually this spell is so powerful that it might have stopped and started again several times and if you were paying attention you might also have noticed that the sky got very dark on at least a dozen occasions and mysteriously you will have travelled forward in time a few weeks. (That's why you've got to be careful that you don't miss your birthday.)

Right-angled triangles

Once you've understood how to crack squares and rectangles you should find right-angled triangles are simple enough too.

To save writing out any numbers, we'll just call the triangle's height "h", and the size of its bottom "b". (Most triangles have more bottom than height, so

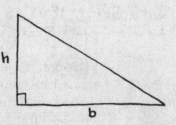

using letters rather than numbers stops them being self-conscious.) You can see why it's easy to work out the area of a right-angled triangle if you get two the same and put them together...

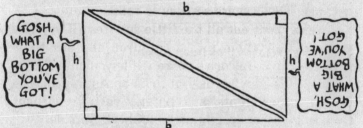

The two together form a rectangle, and to get the area for the two of them you can just multiply the height of this rectangle by the width. So if the area of *two* triangles is the height times the base, you can see that the area of *one* triangle is *half* the height times the base ... or:

$$\text{Area of triangle} = \tfrac{1}{2} \times \text{height} \times \text{base} = \tfrac{1}{2} \times h \times b = \tfrac{1}{2}hb$$

The joy of right-angled triangles is that all you do is measure the two short sides. (One will be the

bottom and one the height, it doesn't matter which.)
You multiply these together then halve the answer
and there you are. Let's find an example to show
you. Aha! That corner-cupboard top looks perfect.

Sorry, Duchess, this will only take a minute.

When we look at the top we find it's a right angle
and the short sides measure 3 m and 1·2 m. All we
do is work out $3 \times 1·2 \times \frac{1}{2}$ and we get an area of 1·8 m².
Gosh! That's the same as the tabletop – which goes
to show that completely different shapes can have
the same area.

Wonky triangles

If your triangle doesn't have a right angle then life gets trickier. These triangles don't have a posh name so we'll just  call them "wonky" and any sort of triangle (equilateral, isosceles or scalene) can be wonky. Here are some of the ways of finding the area of a wonky triangle:

- **Geometry.** This involves making a really accurate drawing and dropping a perpendicular, then bisecting it and creating a rectangle which you measure with dividers providing you haven't got any cocktail sausages stuck on them. Although this is rather good fun, it can be quite dangerous (if you accidentally drop the perpendicular on your foot it can break several small bones) so we'll leave this rough stuff for another book.

- **Trigonometry.** Here you need to know the lengths of sides and the precise angles and then use formulas such as Area $= \frac{1}{2}bc(sinA)$ but then you also have to know that "*sin*" is short for "sine" which seems a bit pointless and doesn't help much if we don't know what sines are so we'll leave that method alone too.

- **Measuring.** That's what *this* book is supposed to be about and luckily it's quite easy because any wonky triangle can be split up into two right-angled triangles, which you can measure and work out.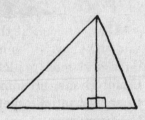

Really silly shapes

As long as a shape doesn't have any curved edges you can always split it into rectangles and right-angled triangles, then measure them up and work them out. Let's find one and show you.

Perfect! Excuse us...

All we need to do is divide the nicely polished tabletop up into rectangles and right-angled triangles, so let's get our dividers and scratch some lines across it.

Ahem ... as we Murderous Maths people are sensitive types we can detect an air of hostility here. How would you feel if we marked our lines with cotton held by Blu-Tack? In the meantime here's some money so you can go and treat yourselves to a curry at the "Ravenous Rajah". It's the least we can do.

All we do now is measure and work out the areas of all five rectangles and add on the four little triangles. Actually there's a slightly cleverer way because if you measure the maximum length of the table and the maximum width, you can see what the area would be if the corners weren't missing. You then work out what size the triangles are at the four corners and subtract them to get an answer – and doing it this way uses less maths.

Why do we measure areas?

The usual reason is that you need to cover an area with something. For instance, you might want to paint your bedroom wall bright pink. In this case you need to know how much paint to buy. On paint tins it tells you how much area the paint will cover, so if your tin says "contents will cover two square metres" and your wall is 6 m², then you know you'll need three tins. The same applies for muck-spreading in fields. You need to know how many hectares one tank-load of muck will cover. Incidentally, if you're buying your paint and muck at the same time don't get them mixed up. Although having a bright pink field isn't too bad, you'll find yourself sleeping in the lounge for months.

Circles

Exact circles are about the only curved shape that you can find the area of easily with a ruler. Although we are going to find an area, you only need to get one measurement which is called the "radius" and then you do a little sum. Let's see if we can find something round to demonstrate.

A round table! Perfect.

It's just not his day, is it?

If you know where the centre of a circle is, you can measure the distance from the centre to the edge. This is the *radius* of the circle or *r* for short. If you don't know where the centre is you've got two choices.

- Put your tape or ruler right across the circle and move it about until you find the longest distance between the two edges. This is called the *diameter* of the circle or *D* for short. If you're being clever you'll have realised that the diameter of a circle is equal to twice the radius, so to get the radius you just divide the diameter by 2.

● Put your tape right round the outside of the circle and measure how far it is round. This is called the *circumference* of the circle and if you are dealing with something like a tree, this is a lot easier than measuring across the middle! Next you need to divide the circumference by "π" which will give you the diameter, then don't forget to divide the diameter by 2 to get the radius.

Yuk! If you haven't seen any other Murderous Maths books, you'll be wondering what's a "π". It's a special number for dealing with circles which is spelt "pi" and pronounced "pie" and is equal to 3·1416. So to make your circumference into a diameter you just divide by 3·1416 and then divide by 2 to get the radius. This is all very well if you're the sort who uses a calculator for everything including counting your toes, but what if you're tough and think calculators are just for wimps? It's a bit unfair having to divide by 3·1416 and then divide by 2 so there's a special trick just for you:

If you multiply the circumference by 0·16 you'll get the radius.

As sums go it's not too bad and there's even an easy method – you multiply by 2 four times then divide by 100. It gives a very close answer and it's a whole lot cooler than being a calculator zombie!

So there we are armed with the radius of our

106

circle. But how do we get the area? There's a little formula which says:

$$\text{Area of circle} = \pi r^2$$

This means that you multiply the radius by itself, then multiply the answer by 3·1416. (Another toughie trick is that instead of the boring 3·1416, you can just multiply by 22, then divide by 7 to get a close answer.)

To see how it all works, we'll look at our round table.

The maximum distance across is 1·5 m, so that's the diameter. When we divide it by 2 we get the radius as 0·75 m. We now use our area formula which tells us that the area of the table = πr^2 which is $\pi \times 0·75 \times 0·75$.

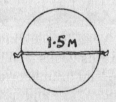

This comes to 1·767 m². Just for fun we'll round this off to two figures and get the amazing result...

Really awkward shapes

IF YOU'RE SO KEEN ON AREAS, HOW BIG IS THIS STAIN?

This area is a bit more awkward to measure because it doesn't have any nice straight edges and not so much as a hint of a friendly right angle. Panic not! There's a simple way to deal with this.

The grid method

What you do is make a grid – in other words a pattern of square boxes – over your shape. If your awkward shape is drawn on paper, you can draw grid lines over it, or if you don't want to make a mark on your original shape, you draw the gridlines on tracing paper then put it over the top. If your awkward shape is on a restaurant floor, then you can mark a grid out on the floor with loads of drinking straws (or lengths of string if you have them).

The secret is to make your boxes a nice helpful size. The smaller the boxes are then the more accurate your answer will be, but you don't want to make too much hard work for yourself. On a small paper drawing you might like the boxes to be 10 mm square, but if you used this size of box on a big curry stain you'd end up with thousands of them. Luckily it turns out that the straws in this restaurant are exactly 200 millimetres long (which is the same as 0·2 metres) so we can use them to mark out lots squares measuring exactly 0·2 m × 0·2 m.

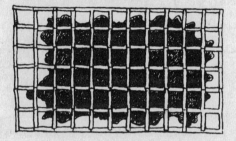

All you do is count up how many squares are inside the shape. In this case you can see there are 31 squares completely inside the shape, so we'll make a note of that in fat letters: **31 complete squares**. There are also 28 squares that are partly in the shape, and here there's two choices:

- Divide the number of "partly squares" by 2, and count the answer as complete squares. This way we get $28 \div 2 = $ **14 more complete squares**. We can add all the complete squares together to get a total of 45 complete squares.
- Look at each "partly square". If more than half of it is in the shape then count it as complete, otherwise ignore it. Here it looks like 14 of them are more than half in the shape, so again we get **14 more complete squares** giving us a total of 45 complete squares.

Now we know that the stain has the same area as 45 complete squares, so all we do now is work out how big *one* square is and it's 0·2 m × 0·2 m which comes to 0.04 m². To get the total area we multiply this by the number of squares and get $45 \times 0.04 = \ldots$

How strange! They don't seem very impressed.

Oh dear! This could be expensive, so we better hurry up and finish this book before we run out of money. On we go then...

WEIGHT AND WHY NEARLY EVERYBODY MAKES A **MASSIVE** MISTAKE

Let's kick off with a quick question: what do you think your weight is? 40 kilograms? 55 kilograms? 197 kilograms? You can get on the bathroom scales and check if you like.

Well, thanks for joining in and getting into the spirit of the occasion, but sadly you're wrong.

To be absolutely correct, your *mass* might be 40 kg, 55 kg or 197 kg, but "weight" is actually the force of your mass being pulled to the ground by gravity. When engineers get fussy they describe weight in units of "kilogram-force" – in other words the force that your scales are feeling from your feet is 43 kgf. If scales were going to be absolutely correct they should be marked in kgf rather than kg.

If you're not sure about this, take your scales on to a rocket and fly into outer space. Now try and stand on them. They will show your weight to be 0 kg!

Yes, there you are floating around your space capsule doing brilliant somersaults and being sick all over the control panel but what happened? Where has your 43 kg gone? Has somebody secretly pumped you up with balloon gas so that you float? Or have your intestines been invaded by space maggots that have eaten all your insides, bones, veins and nerves and just left a tiny shell of skin?

No, don't panic. Your *mass* is still 43 kg because mass is a measure of the amount of stuff that you're made out of. However, when there is no gravity there is no force pulling you down so your weight (which is what the scales measure) is zero.

Now that we've sorted that out, we don't want to seem aloof or precious so we'll go back to referring to mass as weight just like everybody normally does, even though it's wrong.

Units of mass (or weight if you like) come in three handy sizes:

- GRAMS (g): this is the pocket size, useful for things like boxes of chocolates and hamsters.
- KILOGRAMS (kg): this is the standard size which gets used for people and bags of fertilizer.
- TONNES (t): this is the giant economy size for battleships and office blocks.

There are 1,000 g in 1 kg and 1,000 kg in 1 t.

How to weigh a dead fly

Weighing big things is simple enough, you just put them on scales or balances. But what if you need to weigh something really tiny?

You need to make your own special scales and what you need is a postcard, a drinking straw, a long pin, and some squared paper. You also need to use the kitchen scales.

The picture just about explains it all. You fold the postcard into three to make the stand and it's best if you stick it to the table with Blu-Tack. Put two little slots in the top of the card, then stick the pin through the middle of the straw and balance it on the slots. Cut a slit in each end of the straw and slide in pieces of paper to make little trays to put your things on. If it won't quite balance, cut some tiny slips of paper and stick them in the higher end of the straw until it will rest exactly level.

The clever bit is making your "weights".

- Take all the pieces of squared paper you have and weigh them on the kitchen scales. Let's say you have 10 pieces and you find they weigh 80 grams.
- Work out how much each piece of paper weighs – in this case it's $80 \div 10$ which comes to 8 g.
- Work out how many squares are on the paper by counting along the top, then counting down the side and multiplying the numbers together. If you get 60×42, then that makes 2,520 squares.
- Work out how much each square weighs! Here it's $8 \div 2,520$ which is 0·00317 g.
- Cut a few squares out of your paper – and these are your weights! It's also handy to have some pieces sized at 2 squares, 5 squares and 10 squares.

All you do now is put the dead fly or baked bean or bogie on to one side of your balance, and see how many squares of paper you need to balance it. If you have a fat maggot that weighs 39 squares of paper, then the maggot weighs 39×0.00317 g which is 0.124 g. That's useful to know, isn't it?

SPANGLED, TANGLED AND DANGLED ANGLES

Whenever two lines meet, you get an angle.

Oh for goodness sake! Luckily here's Veronica Gumfloss in her spangled tights all ready to do her ballet exercises, so she can demonstrate some angles for us.

At the moment her legs are together, so the angle between them is zero. Now while Veronica goes through her poses, we'll watch what her legs do.

116

The most common angle you come across is the right angle – there's even four of them around the edge of this page because that's what the corners are. As Veronica has shown us, angles smaller than right angles are called "acute" and angles bigger than right angles are "obtuse" and you can even get inside-out angles called "reflex" angles.

Angles are usually measured in degrees, which have a little sign like this ° and there are 90° in a right angle. If you put two right angles together, you

117

can see that 180° makes a straight line. If you put four right angles together you get a full circle, which is 360°.

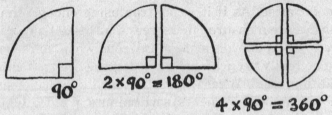

$$90°$$ $$2 \times 90° = 180°$$

$$4 \times 90° = 360°$$

How to make an angle of one degree
As you might imagine, an angle of one degree is really tiny, so here's an experiment to give you an idea how small it is. You'll need about 2 m of cotton, and what you do is loop the middle round your left little finger, then hold your left arm out to the side. Gather up the two loose ends with your right hand, then pinch the two strands together between your right thumb and forefinger and hold them in front of your face.

The angle between the two strands will be about 1°. Not a lot is it? Mind you, the next time you're having 359 friends round for the afternoon, you could all make angles of 1° out of cotton and then all get together in the middle and make a complete circle. There again, you'll probably all end up in a knotted heap of tangled angles. What fun.

How old is a right angle?

Don't panic, you're not supposed to be able to answer this question, but it's easy to see how it might arise. As if it wasn't confusing enough that angles are measured in degrees – just like temperature – it gets even more murderous when you need to be really accurate because degrees are split into 60 "minutes". What's worse is that for ridiculously accurate measurements, each minute of a degree is split into 60 "seconds".

This means that in a right angle there are 5,400 minutes, or 324,000 seconds.

Common angles and special triangles

Apart from right angles, about the only angles you normally come across are 30°, 45° and 60°. These turn up in special sorts of triangles like this:

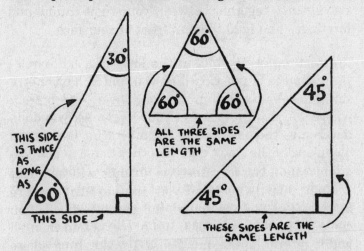

By the way, if you measure the three angles in a triangle and add them up you always get 180°.

There's a neat way of showing this – cut a triangle out of paper, then tear off the corners. Put them together and you get a straight line!

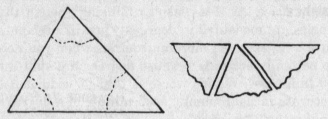

Measuring angles

When it comes to measuring angles you need a *protractor*.

Protractors are usually in the form of a half-circle-shaped piece of plastic which you find in a geometry set. There's a point in the middle at the bottom where you put the point of your angle. All you do is make sure the base line of the protractor is running along one of the lines, and the other line will point to a reading on the side which is the size of your angle.

There are usually two sets of numbers on a protractor. You have to use a bit of common sense to see which one you read from. Obviously if your angle is less than a right angle the number of degrees is less than 90, and if it's more then you need to use the bigger number. It's all quite simple.

The only time you have to watch out is when you're measuring reflex angles.

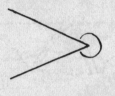

TO MEASURE THIS ANGLE...

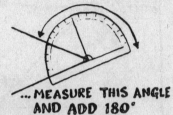

... MEASURE THIS ANGLE AND ADD 180°

You need to put your protractor like this and then don't forget to add the extra 180° to your reading.

Finding your way

One of the main uses for angles is for describing a "bearing" which is what direction you need to go in. Compasses are often marked like this:

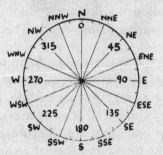

What you do is turn your compass around so that the needle (which always points north) is over the "N" on the compass. A bearing of 0° means directly north, and 180° is directly south. In the old days sailors used to give bearings like "west by south-west", and if you look at the compass you can see that would be a bearing of $247\frac{1}{2}°$.

121

FAZOOSH! Oh no, what's happening now? All of a sudden you are blindfolded and seem to be standing on the edge of a cliff. You feel a fresh breeze tickle your neck, which brings with it a foul sprouty smell.

"Har har!" shouts a distant voice.

"Oh not you again!" you reply. The smell and the "har har" are all too familiar. It's the evil Professor Fiendish, with another diabolical mathematical trap.

"Stand perfectly still!" he snarls. "I've transported you to the far end of a very thin line of rock high above a raging sea."

"Ooh lovely," you reply. "Is there anywhere to buy a postcard?"

"You won't be quite so smug in a minute!" comes the answer. "At the moment you are facing down the narrow path that leads back to the clifftop, but just one step in the wrong direction will send you plummeting to your doom!"

Overhead you hear the seagulls circling. Doubtless they've seen this trick before and know that

soon there could be a juicy meal served to them on the rocks. Gulp!

"Don't worry!" sneers the professor. "All you have to do is walk straight down the path and you're free, but just to make it interesting – first I'm going to spin you around!"

You hear footsteps approach and the smell gets worse. Suddenly your elbows are grabbed by two rough hands.

"So how far round are you going to spin me?" you ask trying not to breathe in.

"As I'm in a good mood, I'll let you choose!" chuckled the professor. "Pick a number between 1 and 500 – and that's how many degrees I'll turn you!"

A few seconds later you are on the clifftop pulling off the blindfold. You look back and see the professor jumping up and down in a mad fury.

"Curses!" he screams in frustration as the gulls vent their disapproval on him with some precision bombing.

But how did you escape?

The answer is that you chose to be spun round 360° – which means you turned one complete revolution. All you had to do was walk forward before the professor realized he had pointed you back in the right direction!

Embarrassing angles

Although degrees are much the most common way to measure angles, there are a few others. Instead of splitting a circle into 360°, very occasionally people split a circle into 400 *grads*. This is so you end up with 100 grads in a right angle which might look neat, but it has never really caught on as an idea. In fact you have to feel a bit sorry for a protractor marked in grads. It must be like turning up to a party dressed in a baby's nappy, only to find it isn't fancy dress.

Angles on the move

If you don't like degrees, there is a completely different way of measuring angles which works like this: suppose you have a circle with a radius of 1 metre, and you mark off a bit of the circumference that is 1 metre long...

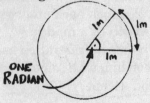

...the angle it makes in the middle is 1 *radian*.

There are about 6·28 radians in a complete circle. You could work this out for yourself if you know about "π" because the circumference of a circle with a radius of 1 metre is 2π metres long which is about 6·28 metres. However, if you don't know about π, you can still tell there are about 6·28 radians by looking at it.

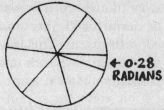

From this you can see that 6·28 radians = 360°.

Radians are used by brainy people for making certain problems easier, but the rest of us needn't worry about them.

Dear Murderous Maths,

That's unfair. You explain what radians are but then you say they only help brainy people. What sort of problems are they solving? Why can't you tell us? Think we're too stupid or something?

Yours sulkingly,
Ernest Whinge.

OK, you asked for it. Radians are especially useful in analysing "angular movement" which means things that are moving round such as wheels, conveyor belts and turbines.

One special radian problem involves pendulums, which are those dangly things you find ticking away in old clocks. Providing it isn't swinging too far either way, a pendulum will always take exactly the same time to move backwards and forwards. This can be proved with maths, but only if you measure the angle of dangle that the pendulum moves through with radians. How's that?

Dear Murderous Maths,

Better.

Yours reassuredly,

Ernest Whinge.

P.S. That's enough about angles. Can we have something else now?

LUMPS, BUMPS AND A QUESTION OF PRINCIPLE

So far we've sorted out how to measure lines with one dimension and areas with two dimensions. We now move into the world of three dimensions, which means that we are measuring *volumes* and here there's bad news and good news.

● The bad news is that the sums get harder. Urgh.
● The good news is that quite often you don't need to do any sums. There is usually a much more fun way to measure volumes because lumps and bumps take up space and what's more you can weigh them.

The sums

Remember we had a rectangular table, and the area was the length times the width (or as the formula says: area of rectangle = ab). We also ended up with answers in m^2.

If you have something with rectangular sides, such as a cornflake packet, then to get the volume you just multiply the height and the width and the length together – in other words you need three measurements. (Don't forget to use the same units for all of them!)

Things with rectangular sides are called "cuboid" and the formula is:

Volume of a cuboid = length × width × height = abc

If the length and the width and the height all happen to be the same, then you've got a "cube", so the volume is just length × length × length or a^3.

We know units of areas are square metres, and luckily volume units are just as easy. Because you are multiplying metres times metres times metres, your answer comes out in *cubic* metres or m^3.

VOLUME = 2 × 3 × 1·5 = $9_m{}^3$

A nasty thought

How many cubic millimetres are there in a cubic metre? We've already seen that there are 1,000,000 square millimetres in a square metre, but now we have to look at this sum: 1 m^3 = 1 m × 1 m × 1 m = 1,000 mm × 1,000 mm × 1,000 mm. If you work it out you find that there are *one thousand million* cubic millimetres in one cubic metre. Of course if you don't believe it, all you have to do is get a block of wood measuring 1 m × 1 m × 1 m, then cut it up carefully into 1,000 slices each way then count the bits. You should be finished by the year 35,007. You'll be ready for a good long bath and a change of clothes by then, won't you?

Oil drums and soup tins

Apart from cubes and cuboids, most other volumes are murderous to work out using normal measurements and sums. Luckily the only common one that anybody has to deal with is a cylinder such as a tin can or an oil drum.

All you do is measure the diameter OR the circumference of the cylinder – whichever's easiest – then work out the area of the base. This is easy enough because it's a circle and circles are all nicely explained for you on page 104. You then measure the height and multiply it by the base area, and there you are – you've got the volume.

No, not quite Pongo. If you use these measurements, the volume you work out tells you how much space the drum takes up. What you need to know is how much space there is *inside* the drum which is called the *capacity*. Usually the walls of tin cans and oil drums are so thin that the capacity is almost the same as the volume, but if the walls are thick then you have to take *internal measurements*.

Finding out the capacity is also easy. You just measure the diameter across the inside and so work out the inside base area, then measure the height inside and multiply them together. All very easy you'll agree, but maybe you'd prefer to try the wet method? It's more fun and best of all it works for any shape of container, even giant rabbit-shaped jelly moulds...

1 Throw away your measurements and go and get a measuring jug and run a hose pipe from the nearest tap.

2 Fill up the measuring jug with an exact amount of water (e.g. 1 litre).

3 Tip the water into the container.

4 Keep filling up the jug and tipping it in. Count how many jugs it takes to fill the container.

In that case the capacity of your drum is 293 litres!

A litre is how "capacity" is usually measured, but if you prefer you can measure capacity in cubic metres. All you need to know is that there are 1,000 litres in 1 m^3. In this case the capacity would be 0·293 m^3.

As Pongo turns the air green, we'll just have another think about litres and cubic metres. As well as being used for capacity, litres are usually used for amounts of liquids because liquids can be any shape you like. If your milkman goes completely potty one day and delivers a milk carton that measures 1 m × 1 m × 1 m, then you will have a cubic metre of milk sitting on your doorstep. It's easy to tell this by looking at it because it's cubic and measures a metre in each direction.

You'll find that it's a bit awkward to carry inside because not only do you have to remove the door frame and some of the wall, but also when you come to lift the carton you'll find it weighs one tonne. By the time you've got it on the kitchen table you'll be ready for a nice cup of coffee which is when your problems really start because you want a dash of milk in it, and so you need to open the carton. Well you know what happens when you open milk cartons ... sploosh! It goes all over the place. You'll have milk all over the floor, across the table, dripping from the ceiling. There will be milk in your shoes and up your nose and oozing out of the radio – in fact the only place where there won't be a trace of milk is in your coffee. It's at this point that you look at the mess and you have real trouble imagining a nice neat cubic metre of milk. For some strange reason, calling it 1,000 litres seems more natural.

The fancy crown

So far we can work out the volume of cuboids or cylinders, but just suppose someone came up to you with a nice shiny crown decorated in leaves all made from solid gold, how would you work out the volume?

This isn't just a made-up problem, this is actually one of the greatest measuring challenges of all time and it happened about 2,250 years ago in a town called Syracuse in Sicily. The story involves theft, deception, cunning, gruesome punishment and a genius detective – i.e. it's just the sort of thing you've come to expect from Murderous Maths, so grab your popcorn and roll the opening titles:

A QUESTION OF PRINCIPLE

☆ ☆ STARRING ☆ ☆

KING HEIRO II... AS THE KING OF SYRACUSE
CO-STARRING **ARCHIMEDES**... AS THE MATHS WIZARD
SPECIAL GUEST STAR: **RIPPOFFEDES** AS THE CHEATING GOLDSMITH
AND INTRODUCING: **DOMESTICITES**... AS THE HAND-MAIDEN

135

137

139

COMING SOON... **PRINCIPLE 2** – THE SEQUEL!

Grapes and elephants

The best thing about the fancy crown story is that it's all about maths but there aren't any numbers in it! What Archimedes realized was that putting something in water is a very good way of measuring the volume and this is even useful for us today. Here's how to measure the volume of something small with an odd shape such as a bunch of grapes:

- Half fill a measuring jug with water – say to the 500 ml mark. (On a measuring jug, "ml" means millilitres, and 1 millilitre is one thousandth of a litre or if you prefer 1 cm^3 or even one millionth of a cubic metre.)

- Put your bunch of grapes in the water, making sure there are no air bubbles. Once again your dividers can come in handy for pushing them down to make sure they are completely under the surface – otherwise you can be boring and use a spoon.

- Note the new level of the water in the jug, e.g. 830 ml.

- Subtract the old level from the new level. In this case you get $830 - 500 = 330$ ml and that's the volume of the bunch of grapes!

If you use some common sense, you can do the same trick with bigger things. Here's how to get the volume of an elephant:

- Put your elephant in a large container such as a big building skip.

- Fill the skip with water until it completely covers the elephant. (You must make sure the elephant is completely submerged so use your dividers to push it under.)

- When the elephant has stopped thrashing around and the water is still, draw a line on the skip where the water level comes to.
- Carefully lift the elephant out of the skip, then hold it above and shake any loose water off into the skip.
- Get your measuring jug and hose pipe. Keep filling up the measuring jug and tipping it into the skip until you reach the level you marked.
- You didn't forget to count how many times you filled up the measuring jug, did you? Providing you counted exactly, you can then work out the volume of the elephant.

And from this you can work out that the volume of the elephant is 6·274378 m³ which is always a handy thing to know.

Something that a lot of people get wrong...
When you're using the Archimedes method of measuring volumes, you have to make sure that the object is right under the surface of the water – then you know that **the volume of displaced water is equal to the volume of the submerged object**. As we've seen, the volume of displaced water can be worked out by seeing how far up the water level goes.

The story of Archimedes and the crown is quite well known, and a lot of people have heard of a thing called "Archimedes' Principle" and so they think this way of measuring volume is Archimedes' Principle. Bless 'em, but they are wrong because they have only heard half the story. Of course we're going to see the second half, but before we do we've got a bit of murderous maths to catch up on.

HOW DENSE ARE YOU?

There's a classic old joke that goes "What weighs more, a tonne of feathers or a tonne of lead?" It's worth trying this question out on somebody, but you've got to pick your moment. It's best if they are busy putting on their lipstick or fixing the washing machine or trying to stop a large dog running off down the beach with their trousers. If you're really lucky you might find them trying to do all three things at once, so you can catch them out and they will say...

Ha ha! Of course, the answer is that they both weigh one tonne, so neither is heavier, which makes you look really clever and them look really silly.

A more interesting question is what takes up more space – a tonne of feathers or a tonne of lead? The answer is that a tonne of feathers takes up a lot more space because feathers have a much lower *density* than lead. If you like, the weight of the feathers is spread out much more, but with lead the weight is all packed in tight together. The difference between density and weight is that weight doesn't care how big a thing is but density does.

Another way of looking at this is that if you have two boxes the same size, one full of lead and one full of feathers, obviously the box of feathers will be lighter. The feathers cannot pack as much weight into the box as the lead can, because they have a lower density.

When it comes to measuring density, water is the easiest thing to deal with because if you weigh 1 litre of water you'll find it comes to exactly 1 kilogram. This means that the density of water is 1 kilogram per litre.

When you know this you can work out what different volumes of water would weigh, a simple example is that 2 litres of water will weigh 2 kilograms and so on. If you have 1,000 litres of water, then it weighs 1,000 kilograms which is exciting because 1,000 litres is 1 cubic metre and 1,000 kilogram is 1 tonne. This gives another neat result: the density of water is 1 tonne per cubic metre, which you can write as 1 t/m^3.

Density comes in very handy for linking up volume and weights. For instance when Pongo made 293 litres of soup, he could have worked out its rough weight because soup is mostly water and the density will be about 1 kg/l, so Pongo's soup would weigh about 293 kg.

Floating and sinking
Just out of interest – anything with a density less than water will float. For instance, most wood has a

density of about 0·8 t/m³ which is less than water at 1 t/m³. That's why it floats!

On the other hand, gold has a density of 19·3 t/m³. So do you think it would float or sink? Of course, it's nearly 20 times denser than water so it hits the bottom with a THUNK and stays there.

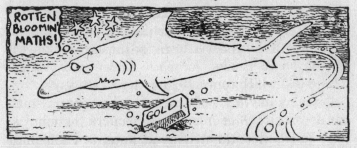

How to work out your own volume

There are some things that only just float – or only just sink very slowly – and those are land animals, including people! This means that the density of humans is very close to the density of water, which gives you a handy way of working out your volume. All you need to do is weigh yourself, but you need the answer in kilograms.

(If your bathroom scales are in old-fashioned stones and pounds, then you need to do this sum: multiply the stones by 14 and then add any odd pounds to get your total weight in pounds. Divide this number by 2·2 to get your weight in kilograms.)

As your density is almost the same as water at 1 kg per litre, your volume is 1 litre for each kilogram you weigh. If you weigh 41 kilograms, then your volume is 41 litres! If you like you can divide by 1,000 to get your volume in cubic metres – in this case it would be 0·041 m³.

This sort of thing is really handy to know if you want to try the old favourite student trick of seeing how many people you can get into a small car. All you do is work out the capacity inside the car which might come to something like 2·3 m³. (You could do this by seeing how many measuring jugs of water you can pour in through the sun roof.) You then work out roughly the volume of each student which might be 65 litres or 0·065m³. All that's left is to divide the space in the car by the space needed for each student, so you get 2·3 ÷ 0·065 which comes to just over 35 students.

It seems like a lot of students to get into a small car doesn't it? Of course, when you pack them in you have to follow a few strict guidelines: no big clumpy boots, oversized earrings, loose clothing, stereo systems or teddy bears, and nobody is allowed to wear a traffic cone on their head or carry a posh-looking briefcase full of toast and comics.

There, have you got them all ready to go in? There's just one more detail to ensure you use up every single tiny bit of space in the car – before the students get in you have to feed them through a mincing machine.

By the way, if our elephant from the last chapter has a volume of 6·274378 m³, then because its density is about the same as water (which is 1 t/m³) it will weigh roughly $6\frac{1}{2}$ tonnes.

Buoyancy

When you put an object in water (or any other liquid), buoyancy is the force that pushes it to the top. As we've seen, if the object is less dense than the liquid then thanks to the way that the buoyancy/density sums work out, there will be enough force shoving upwards to make it float. However, if you put in an object that is denser than the liquid, there isn't enough force to make it float. The important point is that the force is still there – it just isn't strong enough! This means that if you are a weight-lifter, life would be easier if you do it under water because the buoyancy force helps you.

The interesting question is: when you put something in water *exactly how much force* is pushing it up? This is where Archimedes' Principle comes in, so to make sure that Murderous Maths readers can put the rest of the world right, here comes...

PRINCIPLE II
THAT SINKING FEELING

STARRING: **KING HEIRO II** - AS THE KING OF SYRACUSE
ALSO STARRING: **ARCHIMEDES** - AS THE MATHS WIZARD
NOT QUITE STARRING: **HIEFEES** - AS THE CROOKED LAWYER
HARDLY STARRING AT ALL: **RIPPOFFEDES** AS THE CHEATING GOLDSMITH

153

There, that's the real Archimedes' Principle...

> **The buoyancy force on an immersed object is equal to the weight of fluid displaced.**

And it's thanks to Archimedes that we can design and build ocean liners and submarines. Of course, the story would have been even nicer if it had this little ending...

...but we just made that bit up.

WHY TIME IS OUT OF CONTROL

The fun thing about time is that it is the only sort of measurement that humans didn't invent. We decided on how long a metre should be, we chose how heavy we wanted kilograms and we picked the number of degrees we thought would be nice in a complete circle and so on. As far as possible we chose these sizes so that the sums would be simple to do but unfortunately time wasn't arranged by us. Instead time was organized by whoever invented the universe and, as it leads to some really murderous maths, they must have a wicked sense of humour.

It wouldn't be so bad if we had just been given one measurement of time to work from but we were given at least three and we can't control any of them.

The main measurement we were given is:

- One **day** which is how long it takes the Earth to spin round once on its axis.

The other two measurements that we try to incorporate are:

- One **year** which is how long it takes the Earth to go right round the sun.

- One **lunar month** which is the time between one full moon and the next one.

All the little bits of time such as hours, minutes and seconds were man-made, but the first job was to get days sorted out.

Early calendars
Some of the first people who tried to organize days into sensible groups were the ancient Babylonians. They concentrated on lunar months, which they decided should last for 30 days even though they really knew that a lunar month was only about $29\frac{1}{2}$ days long. This odd half-day meant that for every two months that passed, the moon would appear one day earlier, which was irritating. What was even more irritating was that they decided on having 12 months in every year which would have been fine if the Earth took exactly 360 days to get round the sun. Unfortunately the Earth insists on taking just over 365 days to get round so the result of the Babylonian calendar was that every few years they had to put in an extra month to keep track of the changing seasons.

The Babylonian method was changed later on by the ancient Egyptians, who tried to make days fit into years rather than months. They tagged an extra five days on after the twelfth month to make a total of 365 days in a year, which worked much better. But because a year has about $365\frac{1}{4}$ days they eventually decided that they better allow for the extra $\frac{1}{4}$. They did this by adding an extra day to every fourth year, and that's how the leap year was invented.

Finally in 45 BC the Romans decided that their own calendar was awful because politicians were shoving in extra days and months whenever it suited them. The emperor Julius Caesar adapted the Egyptian calendar and organized the twelve months as we know them now with the extra day in leap years being added on to the end of February. Caesar also organized weeks that lasted for seven days and he even changed the name of the month "Quintilis" to "Julius", after himself. (We call it "July" now.) The next emperor also fancied the idea of having a month named after himself, so it won't exactly surprise you to learn that he was called Augustus.

Incidentally – the month January is named after "Janus" who was the Roman god of doorways so the idea is that in January we are stepping through into the new year. The rather cool reason that Janus gets a mention is that he had two faces, one to look back at the old year and one to look forward to the new.

The missing days

Although it lasted for over 1,600 years, even Julius Caesar's calendar couldn't cope with the measurements that nature provides us with. The trouble is that it relies on a year being exactly $365\frac{1}{4}$ days, which is about 11 minutes and 13 seconds too long and in 1582 the Pope realized that dates had fallen

10 days behind where they should be. Pope Gregory XIII (as he was called) decided on two things.

- We didn't need quite as many leap years.
- We needed to catch up on the 10 missing days.

The first problem was solved by saying that you have a leap year every 4 years *unless the year divides by 100*. BUT *you do have a leap year if it divides by 400*. This is why 2000 was a leap year, but 2100, 2200 and 2300 won't be. So if anybody invites you to a mega party on 29 February 2300, don't bother turning up because they are joking.

The second problem was much more fun because to catch up with the correct date everybody needed to skip 10 days, which meant jumping from, say, 1 April to 12 April. (Yes, that does make 10 days missed out! Count them: 2,3,4,5,6,7,8,9,10,11). It was pretty scary to a lot of people.

Although all the Catholic countries did what the Pope said straight away, others took longer to join in. Britain didn't catch up until 1752, and by that time we had to skip 11 days because we'd had a leap year in 1700 when we shouldn't have done. We moved straight from 2 September to 14 September – so if you're doing history, don't fall for this one...

You might think that missing out 11 days made 1752 a bit short but it was still a lot longer than 1751! Up until then Britain had always started a new year on 25 March rather than 1 January, so the last day of 1750 was on 24 March and the following day was 25 March 1751. However, to fit in with everyone else, the British Calendar Act of 1751 stated that 31 December would be the last day of 1751 and 1752 would start on 1 January. Consequently the year 1751 was 83 days shorter than normal.

Why is a leap year called "leap" year?

If your birthday comes on Tuesday this year, then next year it would normally be on a Wednesday. However, if there's a leap-year day (i.e. 29 February) in between your birthdays, then you "leap" a day and your birthday will skip from Tuesday to Thursday.

Is our calendar accurate now?

No. Although we almost have the correct number of leap years, every 3,225 years we need to put in one extra day and even that won't be exactly right! Of course, it doesn't help that the Earth is spinning slower and slower which makes each day about 0.00000002 of a second longer than the day before, so sometimes we take really drastic measures. At exactly midnight on 31 December 1989 they added one *leap-second* before 1990 started! It makes you think that whoever it was that did invent the universe must be having a right old laugh at us trying to work it out.

Other calendars

Pope Gregory based his calendar on the Christian religion, but other religions have their own systems. Muslims use the Islamic calendar and Jews use the Hebrew calendar, both of which are based on the lunar month of between 29 and 30 days, and both systems have ingenious ways of adding in extra leap-days or leap-months when they need to. The ancient Aztecs had an even fancier system which mixed up the 365 day year with a 260 day religious calendar. It used to take exactly 52 normal years to get through 73 religious years and each time this happened they celebrated by sacrificing somebody, then splitting open the victim's chest and lighting a fire in it. Good old Aztecs, anything for a laugh eh?

Measuring time and talking Latin

Now that we've sorted days out, we can see how humans divided parts of the day up and it works like this:

- 24 hours in one day
- 60 minutes in one hour
- 60 seconds in one minute

We usually split the 24 hours into 12 hours in the morning and 12 hours in the afternoon. The time in the middle is called "noon" and if you can see the sun, that's when it is highest in the sky (this position is called the "meridian"). If you ever refer to nine o'clock in the morning as "9 a.m." did you realize you were talking in LATIN? The Latin word for "before" is "ante", so 9 a.m. is short for 9 o'clock *ante meridian*. As the Latin word for "after" is "post", when you refer to nine o'clock in the evening as 9 p.m. what do you think "p.m." stands for?

Digital clocks don't like having to bother showing "a.m." or "p.m." so instead a lot of them have a "24 hour" display. Times in the morning look much the same – e.g. 7:15 a.m. looks like 07:15 – but in the afternoon 4:45 p.m. would become 16:45. If you aren't used to times like 16:45, all you do is take 12 away from the hours number and that way you can see that it's 4:45 p.m.

The odd thing about clocks

It's obvious what the time is when you're looking at a digital clock, because it just lists the hours then the minutes and then it might also tell you the seconds:

Here the time is 13 seconds past 28 minutes past 22 hours. Of course the "22" is telling us that it's long past noon, so if we subtract 12, we find that the time is 28 minutes and 13 seconds past 10 at night.

If you want to know more about time and especially about old-fashioned clocks you can find it in *Murderous Maths*, but as this book is about measuring things you should know that there's something rather strange about the way normal clocks show the time. Suppose you have a ruler with lines on it, the lines can only mean one thing such as centimetres or millimetres. However the lines and numbers on a clock have completely different meanings depending on which hand is pointing at them!

The numbers only tell you what hour is involved and so the little hour-hand is the only one which uses them. In this case the hour is about "2".

The big hand is close to the 11, but as this is the minute hand we have to ignore the numbers. More important are the little lines between the numbers, because with the minute hand they represent the minutes. Usually clocks don't put any numbers by the little lines, you just have get used to how many minutes they represent. In this case you can see that it is just 4 minutes before the hour, i.e. 4 minutes to 2.

And finally – stay calm

If there is another big hand that you can see moving, then this will be indicating the seconds ticking away. This hand uses the same little lines as the minute hand, but this time instead of representing minutes, the lines represent seconds. The seconds are not labelled and there is no warning sign or anything so you just have to remember this vital point: *the hand that you can see moving is the second hand*. It's worth repeating this hundreds of times to yourself to make absolutely sure you are fully aware of it, or the consequences could be murderous.

Oh really? Just imagine forgetting what the second hand is for. You might suddenly think that the second hand is showing the hours instead. Gosh – that means you would end up seeing your life ticking away at the rate of 12 hours every minute! That's about one month every hour – and so this time tomorrow you'll be two years older and in 12 months you'll be over 730 years old.

Who looks silly now, eh? Don't say you weren't warned.

FROM WATTS TO WEATHER

So far we've had length, areas, volumes, densities, angles and time, but of course nearly everything else can be measured too. Here's a guide to how different things might be measured and what they are measured in.

SPEED
Speed tells you how fast something is moving. If you want to measure how fast somebody can run, you need a watch and you need to know the distance they are going to travel.

To work out the speed you divide the distance by the time they took. In this case you get

$$\text{Speed} = \frac{\text{distance}}{\text{time}} = \frac{100 \text{ metres}}{42 \text{ seconds}} = 2.38 \text{ metres per second}$$

If you want to convert m/s (which is the short way of writing metres per second) to kilometres per hour, you just multiply your m/s speed by 3·6. In this case 2·38 m/s becomes 8·57 km/h. If you want to know where the 3·6 comes from, speed has a whole chapter to itself in *More Murderous Maths*.

Of course there are other ways of measuring speed. If you're in a car you can read the speed from the speedometer, and if you are a traffic policeman you can stand at the side of the road with a thing like a ray gun, which can tell you how fast any cars or high-speed grannies are going past you.

TEMPERATURE

You usually measure temperature with a thermometer, although for very hot things or very cold things you might have to use some fancy electrical gear. Temperature is measured in degrees and usually we use the "Celsius" scale which is indicated with a "C". Like a lot of things in measuring, Celsius is based on what happens to water, and so it was decided that the temperature that water freezes at is 0° C and the temperature that water boils at is 100° C. Your blood temperature comes somewhere between these two at about 37° C. Nuclear reactions produce temperatures that go up to millions of degrees, but the very very coldest you can get is called "Absolute Zero" and is equal to *minus* 273·16° C.

If you get into serious physics, then instead of Celsius you use degrees in "Kelvins". 0° K is absolute zero, and water freezes at 273·16° K. In other words, Celsius is the same as Kelvins but 273·16° warmer.

By the way, if you have a sadistic team coach who says things like this, then watch out:

COME ON OUT YOU WIMPS— I PROMISE YOU THE TEMPERATURE IS 30 DEGREES!

If she's talking in Celsius then you've got a nice day. If she's talking Kelvins then you won't be able to breathe because all the air will be lying around the ground frozen into solid lumps.

Other units
There are tons of other sorts of things you can measure but as a lot of them are rather specialized, this is just a guide to a few of them.

FORCE
This is measured in **newtons**, after Isaac Newton who first described it accurately. If you have a little 1 kg rock floating in space doing nobody any harm, and you decide to start pushing it with a force of 1 newton, its speed will increase by 1 m/s for every

second you push it. This means that after ten minutes your 1 kg rock will be going at 600 m/s which is 2160 km/h. In fact your little rock has suddenly become quite lethal, and it's all your fault.

PRESSURE

This is the amount of force pushing against an area and this is what you have to deal with when you're blowing up tyres, diving to the bottom of the sea or studying changes in atmospheric pressure. Different situations use all sorts of different units with different names such as torrs, pascals, atmospheres and millimetres of mercury, but they can all be converted to describing the number of newtons you've got pushing against each square metre.

POWER

It wouldn't be fair to have a section on units without mentioning **horsepower** because it's such a good name. This is an old-fashioned measure of power based on what they thought a horse could do and in modern units they reckon a horse could raise $4\frac{1}{2}$ tonnes up one metre in a minute. This is a bit like having 12,000 tins of beans on the floor and giving the horse one minute to put them all on the table.

ELECTRICITY

This involves three main things: **volts** is how likely you are to be zapped, **amps** means how hard you are being zapped and **watts** comes from multiplying volts by amps and is a measure of how brightly you will be glowing if you do get zapped. By the way, you might be interested to know that there are 760 watts in one horsepower. This is a bit sad because it means that your average electric kettle is as powerful as three horses.

FREQUENCY

This is measured in **hertz** (or **Hz**) and is how often something happens in one second. The most common place you'll come across this is with a stereo system, because the sound is made by your speakers vibrating backwards and forwards. If they vibrate 40 times per second (i.e. at 40 Hz) then you hear a very low note. At 1,000 vibrations per second (1 kilohertz or 1 kHz) you hear a medium note such as someone singing, and sounds at 15 kHz are about the highest you can hear. Because light is also made of vibrations, different colours can be described in hertz but luckily our eyes don't worry us with this. If your eye saw some light waves vibrating at 700,000,000,000,000 hertz they would just tell you that it looks blue. Thank goodness!

SOUND

The amount of noise you can hear is measured in **decibels** (or **dB**) and the way this scale works is that if you increase the volume by 10 dB, the sound is twice as loud. A normal conversation is around

65 dB and a motorbike going past might be 110 dB. Anything over 130 dB will start to ruin your ears and if you don't believe it then ask anyone who was standing at the front of The Who's concert at Charlton Athletic Stadium on 31 May 1976.

SO HOW LOUD WAS THE CONCERT?

EH? WHAT?

LIGHT

The brightness of light you can see is measured in **candelas**, and this used to be based on how bright a candle was. Do you want to know what a candela is now? Really? Oh go on then. One candela is the amount of light with a frequency of 5.4×10^{14} Hz and a power of $\frac{1}{683}$ watt that you get in a cone of one steradian. In other words grab a torch, take out the electrics, shove in a candle, shine it in your face and that's a candela.

WIND

Wind can be measured using an "anemometer" which is a little spinny thing with cups on it that gives you the wind speed in mph or km/h. What is more fun is the system called the **Beaufort scale** which was designed so that you can give an indication of wind speed just by looking at things around you. "0" on the scale is absolutely no wind at all, and "1" on the scale is just about enough to disturb a thin trail of smoke.

By the time you get to "4" there's enough wind to move litter and leaves around, "6" makes for big waves at sea, "9" starts pulling your roof tiles off and "12" means you're in big trouble. After that you move off the Beaufort scale into hurricanes which start at strength "1" for 120 km/h winds to a maximum of "5" which top 250 km/h.

RAIN

Weather people love measuring rain and the results are given in millimetres. If you want to have a go, all you do is leave a glass outside to collect any water that falls – which includes rain, snow, dew or hailstones. The bigger the glass, the better it is but it must have sides that go straight up like a tin can. Every day you measure the depth of water in the glass and that tells you how many millimetres of rain you've had. Weather people get really excited if there's more than about 20 mm in their glasses, because that means it's been chucking it down.

WOW!
28MM!

CURRY

The strength rating depends a great deal on location. At the "Ravenous Rajah" curry house in Lower Rumblings the mildest is the Korma and then it increases in strength levels through the Bombay, Madras, Vindaloo and Phal to the House Special which you have to eat straight from the pan because it melts the plates.

THE SADDEST MEASUREMENT OF ALL

There's one final bit of measuring to do and all you need to do it is your finger and thumb. Squeeze the right-hand side of this book and judge for yourself – how many pages would you say we've got left? Yes, sadly there's just the one so soon we'll have to leave the mad, mental and usually misunderstood world of murderous maths. Before we go our various ways though, here's one tip that will help you with EVERY calculation you ever do, whether it's dead simple or simply deadly.

Before you start splashing numbers and decimal points and dividing signs and everything else all over the place SIT BACK FOR A MINUTE. Take a deep breath, rub your eyes, stick your finger inside your shoe and give your foot a little scratch. Then, HAVE A ROUGH GUESS AT THE SORT OF ANSWER YOU MIGHT EXPECT.

It's really worth it – especially if you've had trouble taking measurements! By the time you've fumbled around with all the numbers and signs involved, you can easily lose track of what you were trying to do in the first place.